# *Logo International*

*Volume 3*

# *Logo International*

*Volume 3*

## *David E. Carter*
## *Editor*

**Art Direction Book Company
New York, NY 10016**

© Copyright, 1990, Art Direction Book Co.

Library of Congress Catalog Card Number. 84-071451
ISBN: 0-88108-060-8

Printed in Hong Kong

Art Direction Book Company
10 East 39th Street
New York, NY 10016

Foreign Distributor:
Hearst International
105 Madison Avenue, New York, NY 10016

This third volume of *Logo International* follows the successful format of the first volumes. However, this book shows all the logos in color. The work was received in black and white from the various designers.

Once the book was put together, a decision was made to produce this book in color. At that time, each designer was sent a copy of the pages of his work, and asked to submit the exact colors for reproduction.

Most responded promptly. However, a few did not give us this data. In most cases, the editor arbitrarily assigned colors to those marks.

My thanks go to each designer represented in this book. Designers who wish to have marks considered for future volumes should submit black and white prints approximately 1½ inches high (unmounted). A list of proper colors should accompany the marks submitted.

Mail to:

Logo International
Art Direction Book Company
10 East 39th Street
New York, NY 10016

The marks shown in this book have been submitted by the various designers. Further reproduction of the marks without permission is prohibited.

**Giancarlo Iliprandi**
Milano
1-223

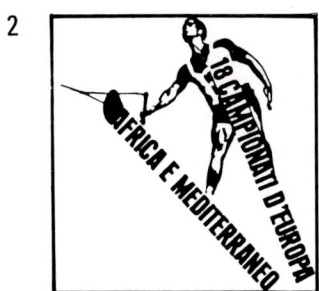
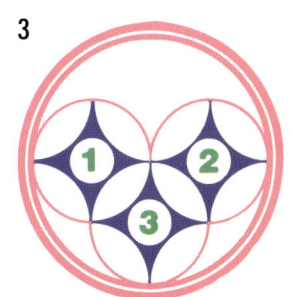
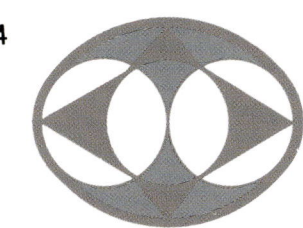

1 Unione Mondiale Di Sci Nautico Gruppo 3
2 Federazione Italiana Di Sci Nautico
3 Unione Mondiale Di Sci Nautico Tre Gruppi
4 Unione Mondiale Di Sci Nautico
5 Unione Mondiale Di Sci Nautico
6 Scinautico
7 Federazione Italiana Sci Nautico
8 Federazione Italiana Sci Nautico

9  Judo Club Jigoro Kano
10 Kendo Club Miyamoto Musashi Milano
11 Kodokan Judo Club
12 Kendo Club Miyamoto Musashi
13 Di Baio Editore
14 Comune Di Milano
15 Rallye Team Valle D' Aosta
16 Edizioni Del Gallo

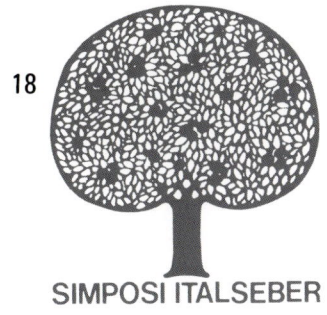
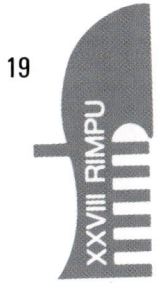

17 RB Rossanna
18 Italseber
19 Rimpu
20 BRW
21 Arflex
22 Arflex
23 Rinaldo Rossi
24 Ala Pubblicita

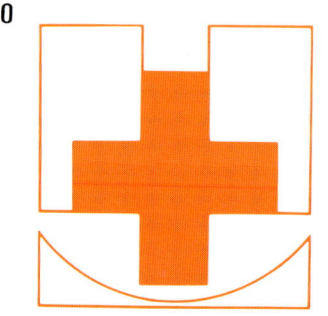
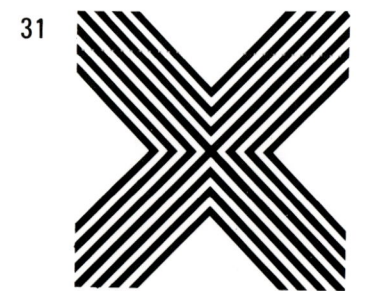

25 Bonati & Beneggi
26 Avv. Prof. Luigi Sordelli
27 Elizabeth Arden
28 San Remo
29 Ankerfarm
30 Ankerfarm
31 Arflex
32 Sci Club Pirovano

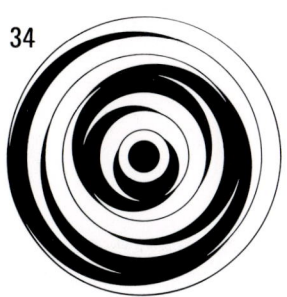

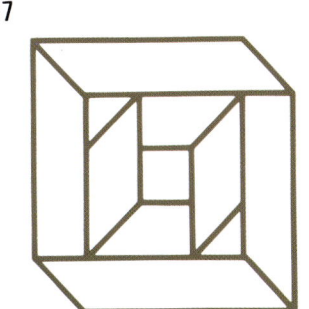

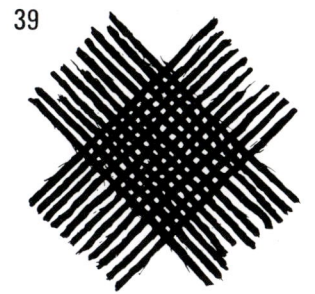
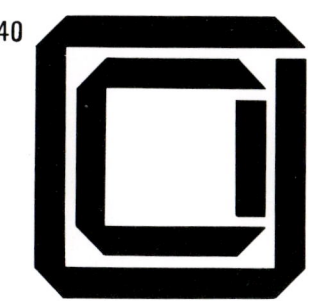

33 Edizioni Del Diaframma
34 Edit Photo
35 Safety
36 RB Rossana
37 Essedi Editrice
38 Isia Di Urbino
39 Comitato Italiano Cotone
40 Giancarlo Iliprandi

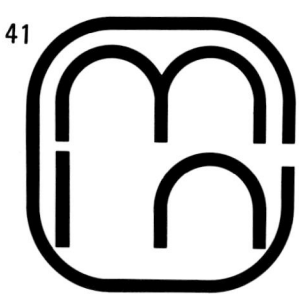 41
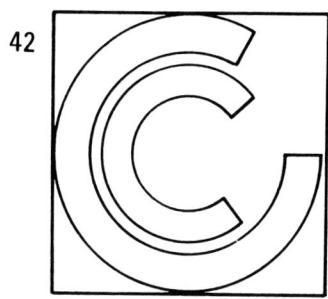 42
 43
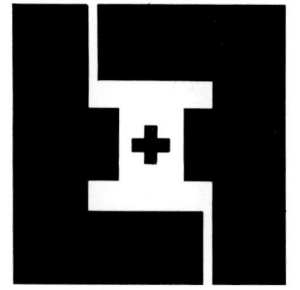 44
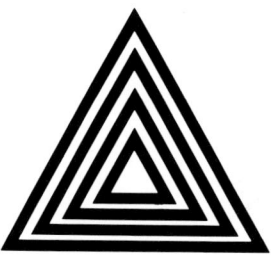 46
 47
 48
 49
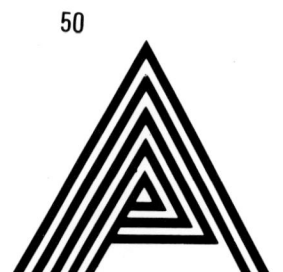 50

41 Comitato Italiano Moda Abbigliamento
42 Comics Club
43 Kunst Haus
44 Ferro & Ferro
45 Italswiss
46 Giannetti Costruzioni
47 Scinautico
48 Arredamenti Errebi
49 Scinautico
50 Rai Radiotelevisione Italiana

51
52
53

54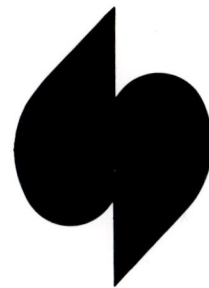
55
56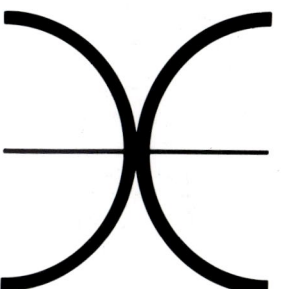

57
58

51 Acciaierie Alfa
52 Villa Arredamenti
53 Stilnovo
54 Editoriale Az
55 Tagliabue Petroli
56 Electa Editrice
57 Freyrie
58 Paridel

59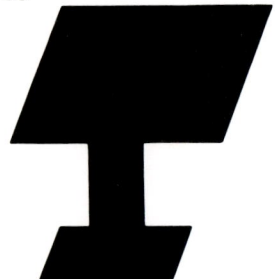
60
61
62
63
64
65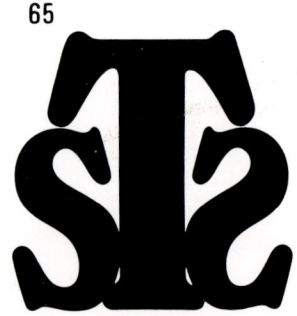
66

59 Teknomeli
60 Zabrinski
61 Editoriale Sciascia
62 Editoriale Sciascia
63 Abitare
64 Abitare
65 Santa Tecla Saloon
66 Longanesi & C.

67

68

69

70

71

72

73

74

67 Centro Italiano Manifestazioni Moda
68 Centro Italiano Manifestazioni Moda
69 RB Rossana
70 RB Rossana
71 RB Rossana
72 RB Rossana
73 RB Rossana
74 RB Rossana

75
76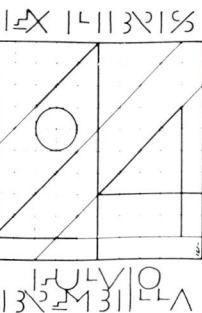
77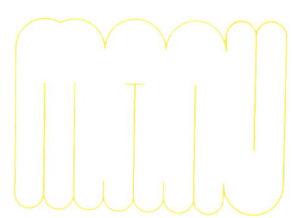

78
79
80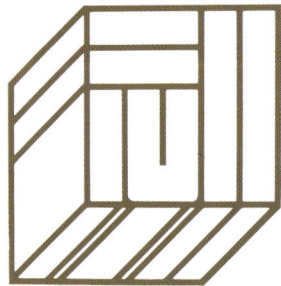

81
82

75 RB Rossana
76 Fulvio Brembilla
77 Manu
78 Ver
79 GMB
80 Full
81 Farmakompas
82 Ministero Per La Programmazione Economica

83

84

85

86

87

88

89

90

83 Essebi Studio
84 Il Diaframma
85 Sci
86 Lola
87 Vog
88 Demapress
89 Rossana RB
90 Teknomeli

91

92

93

94

95

96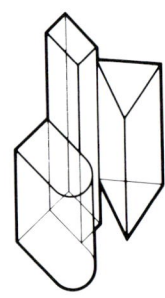

97

98

91 Vog Casa
92 Lotus Casa
93 Edit Photo
94 Dacron
95 Gruppo Editoriale Electa
96 Unione Internazionale Architetti
97 Croff Centro Casa
98 Croff Centro Casa

99

100

101

102

103

104

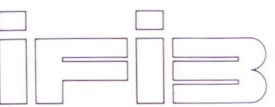

105

106

 99 Dogle's Gallery
100 Cini & Nilis
101 Sispro
102 Norway
103 Organizzazione Propaganda Diretta
104 IFIB
105 I Masters Dell'Arredamento
106 Ribbon

107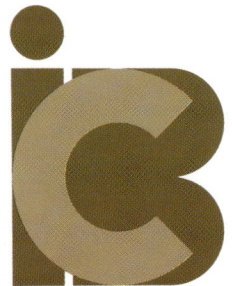

108

109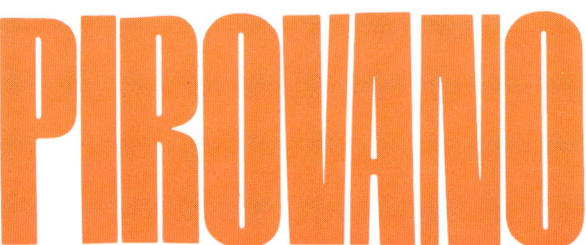

110

111

112

107 Industria Confezioni Belluno
108 Stanley Works
109 Pirovano
110 Freyrie
111 Judo Club Jigoro Kano
112 Associazone Italiana Diffusione Kendo

113

# Dogle's gallery

114

ARGONPLAY

115

ART/DIRECTION '66

116

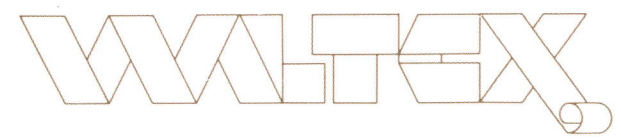

117

**SCINAUTICO**

118

POPULAR
# PHOTOGRAPHY ITALIANA

113 Dogle's Gallery
114 The Argon Service
115 Art Directors Club Milano
116 Waltex
117 Scinautico
118 Edit Photo

119 MILANO CASA OGGI

120

121

122 SUONO

123 cotone

119 Di Baio Editore
120 La Rinascente
121 La Rinascente
122 Edit Photo
123 Comitato Italiano Cotone

124 **PAGINE GIALLE**

125 **INTERNI**

126

127 il diaframma

128 COSMESI

129 ARBITER

124 Seat
125 Gruppo Editoriale Electa
126 Phototeca
127 Edit Photo
128 ETA Editrice
129 L' Editrice

130 **BRERaRTE**

131 **iMASTERS** dell'arredamento

132 *Argomenti*

133 Rivolta

134 *i cicuttini*

135 Teknomeli

130 Brerarte
131 I Masters Dell'Arredamento
132 Argomenti
133 Rivolta
134 I Cicuttini
135 Teknomeli

136 ZABRINSKY

137 COLLEZIONE TECHNIFORM

138

139

140 LOTUS

136 Zabrinsky Point
137 Arflex
138 Arflex
139 Consul
140 Lotus

141

143

144

146

142

145

147

148

141-148  RB Rossana

149 **Palazzini**

150 **VALENTINA**

151 **INDESIT**

152 *sanRemo*

149 Palazzini
150 Vog Casa
151 Indesit
152 San Remo
153 Mercoledi Club
154 L'Arte Degli Estensi
155 Courmayeur
156 Cadran Solaire

157

158

159

160

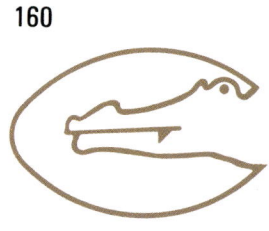

161

162

163

164

165

157 Lo Chalet
158 Papier
159 Le Bien Faire
160 Savinelli
161 Serapian
162 Amga Ferrara
163 I Negozi D' Oro
164 Luci
165 Internazionale Marmi E Macchine Carrara

166

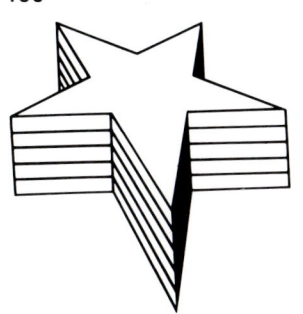

167

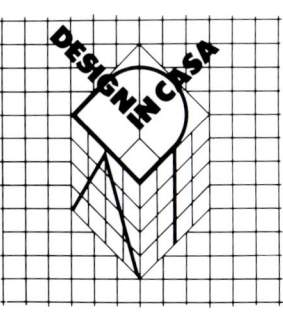

168

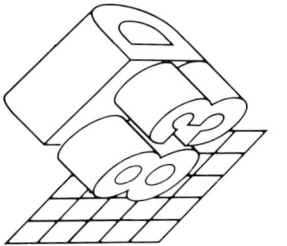

169

170

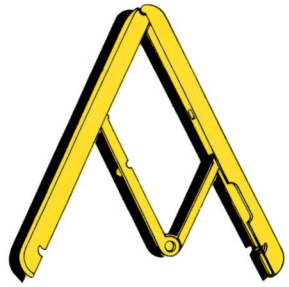

171

172 ADI

173

174

166 Tecnotel
167 Adi-Tecnotel
168 Icsid Design
169 Adi
170 Adi
171 Adi
172 Adi
173 Zeus Pictures
174 Casa Arredo

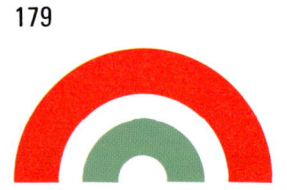

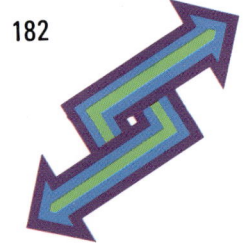

175 Fatro
176 Altur
177 Honeywell Information Systems Italia
178 Grancasa
179 Made in Italy
180 Ardena
181 Gruppo Area Pelle
182 Seat
183 Itaturist

184

185

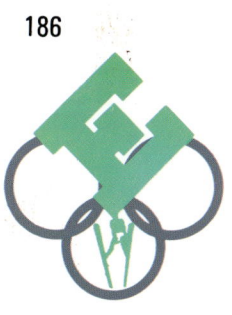

186

187

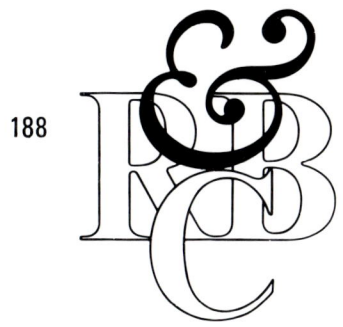

188

189

190

184 Azienda Energetica Municipale
185 Societa Pubblicita Editoriale
186 Federazione Italiana Sci Nautico
187 Esquire & Derby
188 RC&B
189 Citta Convenienza
190 Fatro

191 **ALTA FEDELTA'**

192 **IL DENTISTA MODERNO**

193

194 **ZETA'S**

195 **SERIGRAFIA**

196 **il poligrafico italiano**

197 *FotodiFiori*

198 *Milano Filati*

191 Edisport
192 Edifarm
193 Grancasa
194 Zeta's
195 Zeta's
196 Zeta's
197 Il Diaframma
198 Milano Filati

199

# Torino notizie

200

# *Bianco*

201

202

203

204

205

206

199 Comune Di Torino
200 La Rinascente
201 RB Rossana Styling
202 RB Rossana Styling
203 RB Rossana Styling
204 RB Rossana
205 RB Rossana
206 RB Rossana

**207** SERAPIAN SPORT

**208** *savinelli*

**209**  SAVINELLI 1876

**210** **Setty**

**211** SLIM

**212** *Smok-set*

**213**  DIAMANTE

**214**  IL TENNIS ITALIANO

207 Serapian
208 Savinelli
209 Savinelli
210 Fatro
211 Hunter Douglas
212 Savinelli
213 Gioielli
214 Edilare

215

216 **MOTOCICLISMO**

217 **AUTOMOBILISMO**

218

219 **METEORAMA**

220 **ITALTURIST**

221 **NOR WAY**

222

223

215 Edisport
216 Edisport
217 Edisport
218 Grancasa
219 Associazione Proprietari Meteor
220 Italturist
221 Norway Valbrembo
222 Publimedia
223 Publimedia

Sudarshan Dheer
Bombay
224–247

224

225

226

227

228

229

230

231

224 P.D. Kothari & Company
225 Strand Book Stall
226 Unitel Communications Ltd.
227 Communicaid
228 Impex Diamond Corporation
229 Kalyani Brakes Ltd.
230 Advertising and Industrial Photographers Association of India
231 Spectrum Tricolor Laboratory

232

233

234

235

236

237

238

239

232 Dr. Pankaj Naram's Herbal Remedies Pvt. Ltd.
233 Stock Holding Corporation of India Ltd.
234 Ketan Brothers
235 Joint Publicity Committee Public Sector Banks
236 Transcargo Pvt. Ltd.
237 Chandigarh College of Architecture
238 Universal Diamonds
239 United Telecoms Ltd.

240

241

242

243

244

245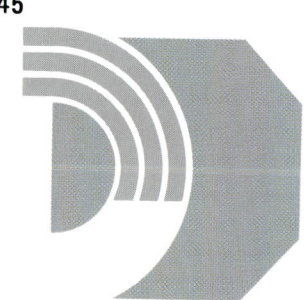

246

247

240 Hindustan Oil Exploration Company Ltd.
241 T.V.S.
242 Kissan Products Ltd.
243 YOGA Thirth Academy
244 Vilaza Hotels
245 Dimexon
246 Devkumar
247 Style Asia Limited

**Mario Narita**
Sao Paulo-Brasil
**248-256**

248

249

250

251

252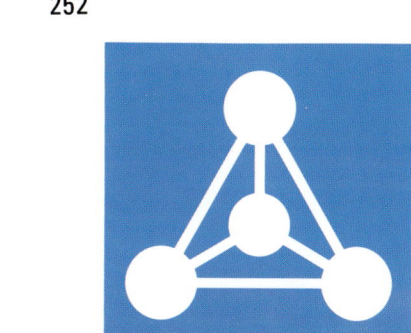

253

254

255

256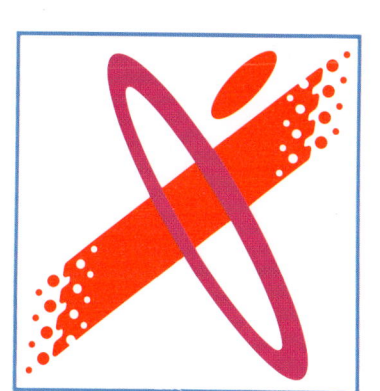

248 Tika Fashion
249 Zanzi Bar
250 CIA. Iochpe Participacoes S.A.
251 Casa Do Pao Queijo Ltda.
252 Alba Quimica Ind. E Com. Ltda.
253 H.L. Restaurantes Ltda.
254 Pojuca Empreend Imentos Ltda.
255 Tip Top Textil Ltda.
256 CIA. Iochpe Participacoes S.A.

**Francisco J. Fernandez Sarasola**
Caracas-Venezuela
**257-283**

257

258

259   260   

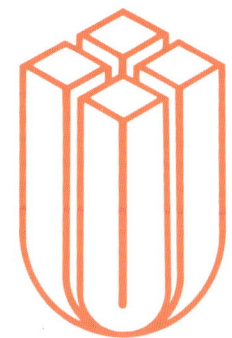

261

262

257  Tecnohipismo
258  Revelado unahora
259  Juegos Deportivos
260  First Trading Innternational
261  Unidiseno
262  Majesty

263 Seguros Capital
264 Typegraf
265 Francisco Fernandez
266 John Fraser
267 Parque de Cristal
268 Centro Comercial Los Chaguaramos
269 Glass Fiber
270 Publiex
271 Instituto de Ensenanza a Distancia
272 Semeze

273

274

275

276

277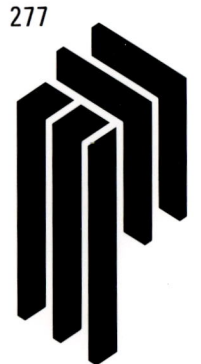

278

273 Segvrosca
274 Inlatec
275 Fundacion Simon Bolivar
276 Fernandez/Lampe
277 Panel Carabobo
278 Haras El Reino

279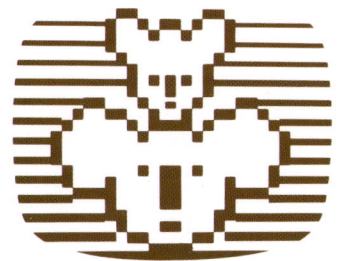

280

281

282

283

279 Koala
280 Los Clasicos
281 Cometa Halley
282 Roser Soler
283 Federacion Venezolana de Remo

**Ricardo Benaim**
Belqique
**284-298**

284

285

286

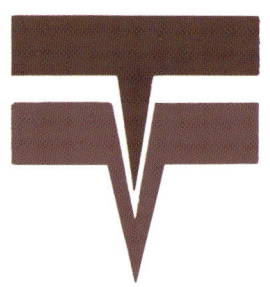

287

288

289

290

284 Shopping News
285 Sillas Sen Sillas
286 Tensaven
287 Otearca Compania
288 Lagosport
289 Seguros La Previsora
290 Sumate

291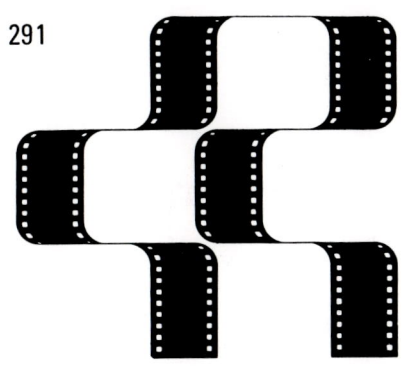
292
293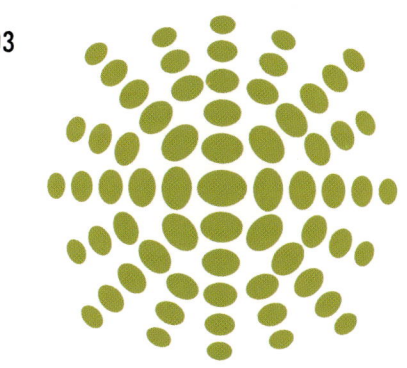
294
295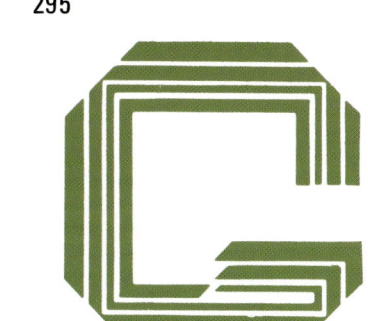
296
297
298

291 Cineautos Nacionales
292 Primer Congreso Venezolano De Neurocirugia
293 Clad
294 Congreso Venezolano De Ciencia Y Tecnologia
295 Desarrollos Guanape
296 Halcon
297 Consucre
298 Playa Moreno

**Aldo Novarese**
Torino, Italy
**299-313**

299

300

301

302

303

304

305

299-304 Societa: Piaggio Milano
305 Divulgo

306

307

308

309

310

311

306-310 Societa Neriolo
311     Urania

312

313

312 Rocca
313 Dieffe

**Nandakishor Kamat**
Kennedy Bridge Bombay, India
314-321

314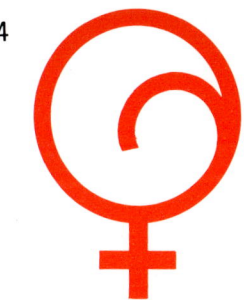

315

316

317

318

319

320

321

314 Gajanan Maternity Home
315 R&D Electronics
316 Swati Power Transmission Pvt. Ltd.
317 Srujan Architects Planners
318 Adventures Screen Printers
319 Span Marketing Pvt. Ltd.
320 All India Flat Tape Manufacturers' Association
321 Parikh & Kulkarni Consulting Engineers P. Ltd.

**Felipe Taborda**
Brasil
322-333

322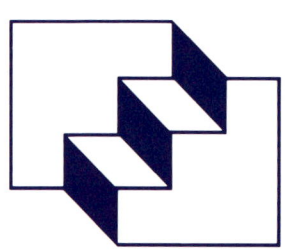

323

324

325

326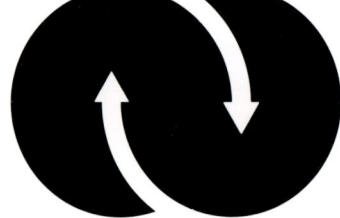

327 

322  Funarte
323  Paralamas do Sucesso
324  Indiscrete Camera
325  The Color of The Sound
326  Pitch Music Productions
327  Black Light

328

329

330

331

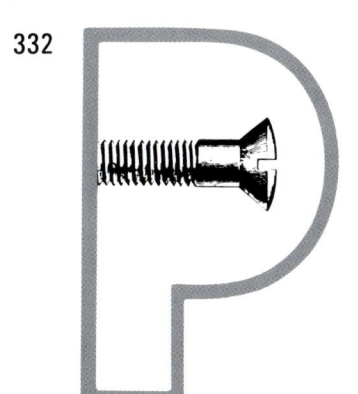

332

333

328 Ceramists Association of Rio de Janeiro
329 Colored Pencil
330 Indiscrete Camera
331 Villas Sportswear
332 Parafuso Clothing Co.
333 Lo Borges

**W. BRAVO**
Sao Paulo, Brasil
334-339

334

335

336 

337

338

339

334 Atleier de Arte W. BRAVO
335 Ellus Ind. E. Com Ltda.
336 Travas Acofort
337 Multi-Sport
338 Tabancura Viajes
339 Haras da Corte

**Signals Design Group**
Vancouver, BC Canada
340-380

340

341

343

344
Neale
Staniszkis
Doll Architects

342

346

340 Curlew Woodworks
341 Rock'n
342 Chilco-Mckeown Productions Ltd.
343 Dragon Boat Festival
344 Neale, Staniszkis and Doll Architects
345 Entertainment Promotional and Technical Associates
346 Savoir Fare Catering

347

348

349

350

351

352

353

354

347 The Pagebrook Hotel
348 The Pagebrook Hotel (Proposed)
349 Vancouver Life
350 Koji Japanese Restaurant
351 Corelli
352 Lacrosse BC
353 Presents of Mind
354 Hi-Tech Rec

355

356 Telsat

357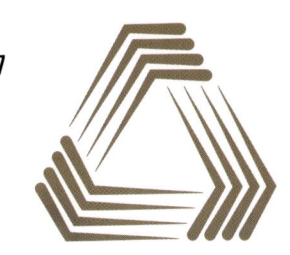

358

359

360

361

362

355 Sagan Information Technologies Inc.
356 Telsat
357 Mitek Corporation
358 British Columbians For Mentally Handicapped People
359 The Rex Chequer Group
360 Westland Management
361 Burnaby Hospital
362 Grandview Resources Inc.

363 6x6x6

364 JEFFERY & CALDER
BARRISTERS AND SOLICITORS

365
MODATECH
*Technology in Style*

366
Security Watch

367

368

369
The A Team

370

371

363 Six by Six by Six
364 Jeffery & Calder
365 Modatech Systems Inc.
366 Security Watch
367 Atlanta Gold Corporation
368 Anchor Gold Corporation
369 The Automotive Team
370 B&C Imp-Ex Corp.
371 Asia Pacific Foundation of Canada

372

373

374

375

376

377

378

379

380

372 Meeting Coordinators
373 Transport Canada Awards
374 Kingman Island
375 RIK Investments Inc.
376 The Beris Group
377 Pareto International Marketing
378 Pelican Cove
379 Sterling Pacific Group Inc.
380 Metropolitan Press (Proposed)

**Gianni Pallotti**
Bologna, Italy
**381-436**

381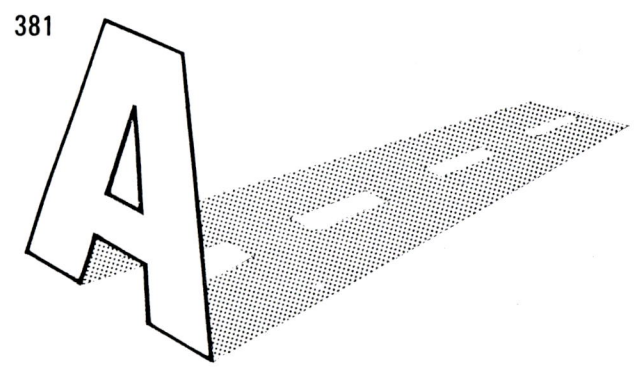

382

383

384

385

386

387

381 Ages Strade
382 Ages Strade
383 Giada
384 Regulus
385 Pulicoop
386 Il Poggio
387 Plurisystem

388

389

390

391

392

393

394

395

388 Urania Borse
389 General
390 Il Poggio
391 Manifatture Brund Mattioli
392 Arnaldo Fini
393 Arnaldo Fini
394 Lea
395 La Ceramica

396

397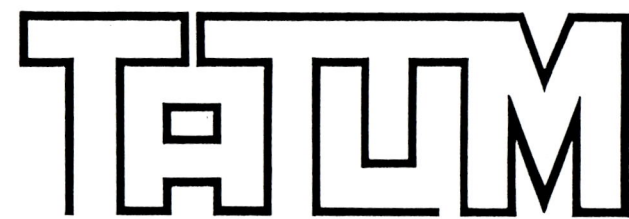

398

399

400

401

402

403

396 Dorica
397 Tatum
398 Team 5
399 Filli Ferrali
400 Quattropi
401 Plurisystem
402 Autorolli Castelli
403 Lelli E Figli

404

405

406

407

408

409

410

404 Gastronomia San Felice
405 Trentini & Morabito
406 Giada
407 Panter
408 Artico
409 Giada Dedositi
410 System Coop

411
412
413

414
415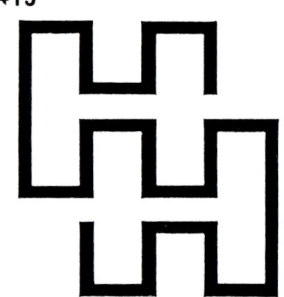
416
417

418
419

411 Trentini & Morabito
412 Trentini & Morabito
413 Liva Beton
414 Liva Beton
415 Hans Hasler
416 Altoreno
417 Moviola
418 Artico
419 Artico

420

421

422

423

424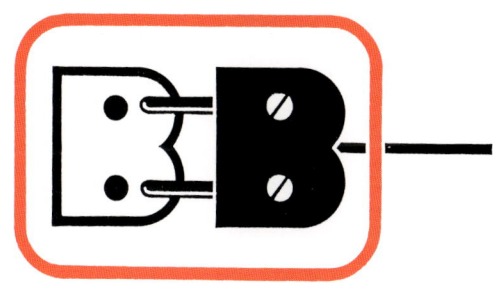

425

426

427

420 Sirio
421 All Services
422 Caress Baby
423 Segre-Bottoni
424 Bruno Benini
425 Cristin Mode
426 Giovannini Giovanni
427 Interarte

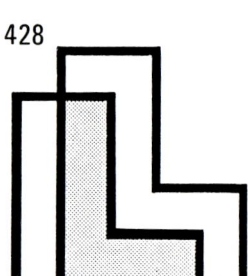
428

429

430

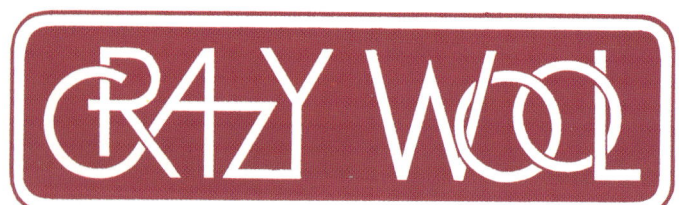
431

432

433

434

435

436

428 Elletre Di Lelli Lino & Figli
429 Lizard
430 Manhattan
431 Crazy Wool
432 La Perla
433 Romana
434 Il Girasole
435 Il Girasole
436 Cristin Baby

**Osmo Omenamaki**
Helsinki
**437–453**

437

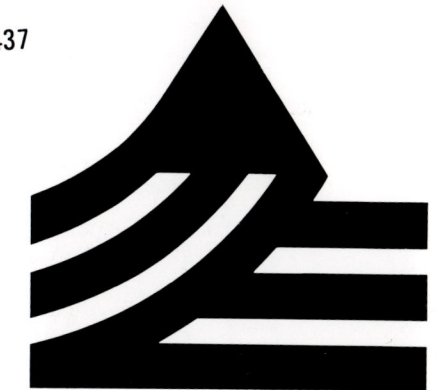

438

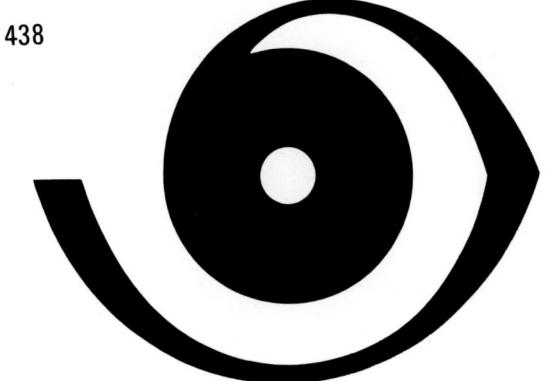

439

440

441

442

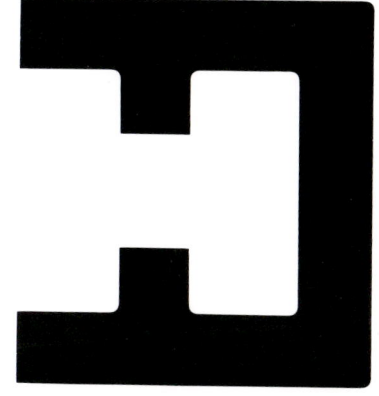

437 Symbol for a Brush Factory
438 Symbol for a Film Company
439 Information Office of the Finnish Dairy Industry
440 SOK Furniture Factory
441 'Kippis'
442 Company Logo for a Construction Company

443
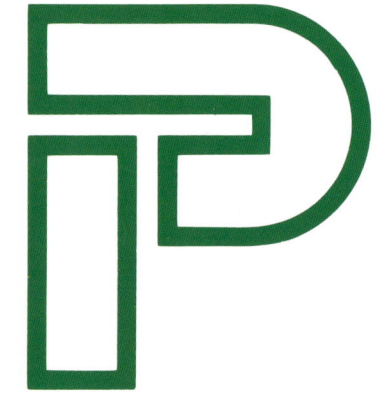

444

445
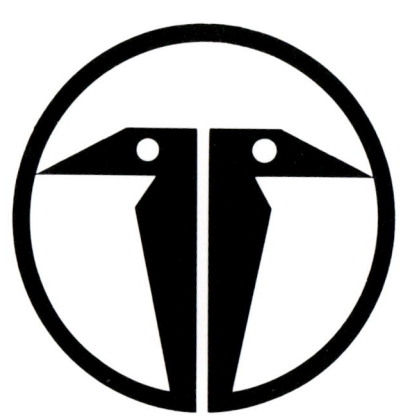

446

447

448

443 Paperitaide
444 Logo for Bookkeeping Company
445 Tikka
446 Logo for a Silk Screen Printing Company
447 Company Logo for a Forwarding Agent
448 Symbol for a Psychiatric Research Foundation

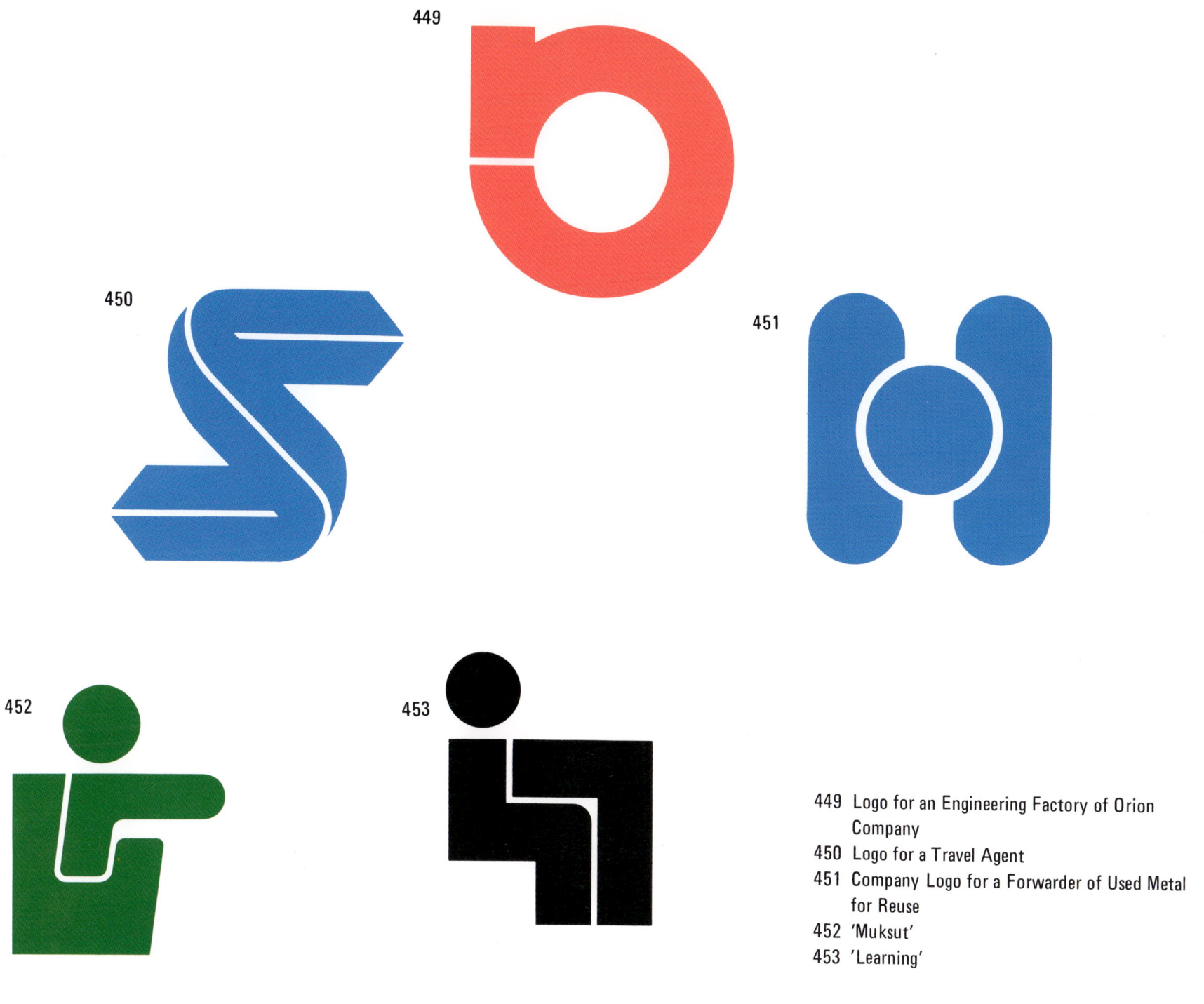

449 Logo for an Engineering Factory of Orion Company
450 Logo for a Travel Agent
451 Company Logo for a Forwarder of Used Metal for Reuse
452 'Muksut'
453 'Learning'

**Rousselot**
S.A. Design, Packaging & Corporate Image
Spain
**454-478**

454

455

456

457

458

459

460

461

462

454 Miras Rousselot, Barna
455 Becover
456 Archivo Documenta
457 Lamaquina
458 Domenech
459 Felicidades
460 Amar Mar Irlanda
461 Cadaque's
462 Michael Doret

**463**

**464**

**465**

**466**

**467**

**468**

**469**

**470**

463  Pan de Pueblo
464  Compania de Tabacos Virginia
465  Grandes de la Pintura
466  Sylvia & Xavier
467  en la mas grande de las fiestas
468  RCP Rilova Casadevall Pedrenosa
469  Eloro De Pizarro
470  Designer, Rousselot

471

472

473

474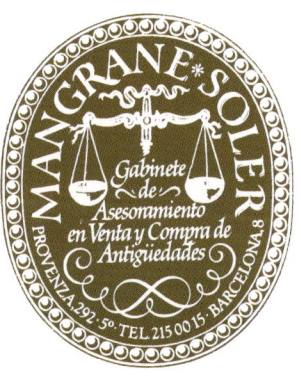

475

476

477

478

471 Rio Grande
472 Frecuencia
473 Felcia
474 Mangrane Soler
475 Julio Bauza
476 Marques de la Ensenada
477 Barcelona
478 Squash

**Armando Ferraro Senior**
Venezuela
**479-490**

479

480

481

482

483

484

479 El Arca Noe
480 Avicola Mayupan
481 La Castanuela
482 Proyeccion 626 C.A.
483 Corina
484 Viva La Papa Restaurant

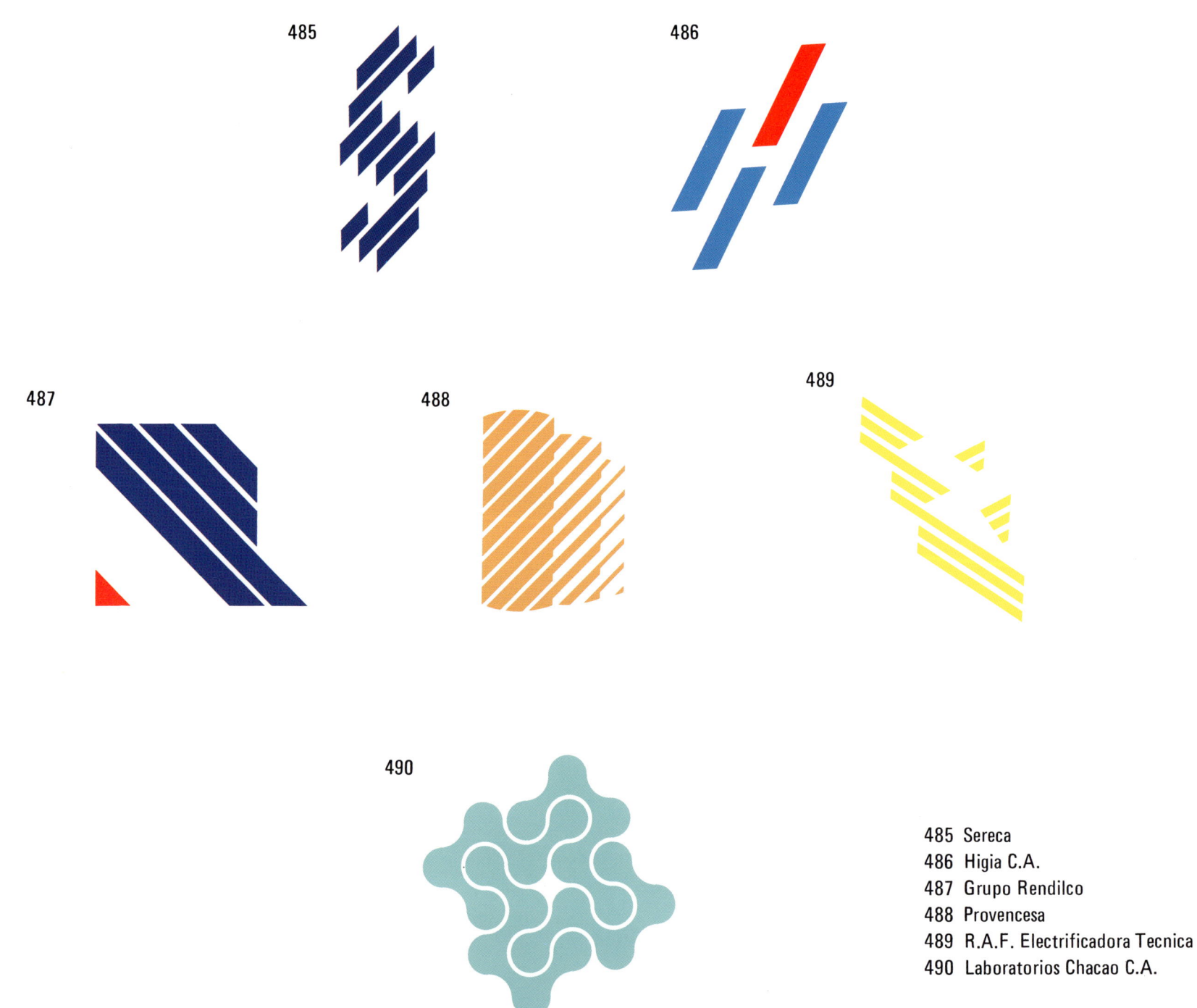

485 Sereca
486 Higia C.A.
487 Grupo Rendilco
488 Provencesa
489 R.A.F. Electrificadora Tecnica
490 Laboratorios Chacao C.A.

**Eduardo Zapata G.**
Mexico, D.F.
**491-555**

491  

492

493 PULIVEX ... (see images)

491  Pulivex, S.A. de C.V.
492  Grupo Helvex
493  Direvex, S.A. de C.V.
494  Plastivex, S.A. de C.V.
495  Funditec, S.A. de C.V.
496  Drafft
497  Helvex, S.A. de C.V.
498  Alta Cocina

499

500

501

502

503

504

505

506

499 Hoteles Mision
500 Confecciones Martin, S.A.
501 IBM de Mexico, S.A.
502 Hoteles Mision/Discotheque
503 Restaurante
504 Estrategias Turisticas, S.A.
505 Asterisco, S.A. de C.V.
506 Constructora

507
508
509

510
511
512

513
514

507 Acabados, Limpieza y Construccion, S.A.
508 Expo/Hort, S.A. Hortalizas
509 Arbol Ideal, Inc.
510 SIEI de Mexico, S.A. de C.V.
511 Campicentro, S.A.
512 McCormack & Dodge de Mexico, S.A.
513 Hortalizas Antonio Urquiza
514 Fotografo

515
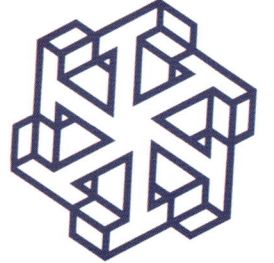

516

517

518

519

520

521

522

515 Turcom, S.A.
516 Pasteleros
517 Intercontinental de Viajesy Servicios Turisticos, S.A. de C.V.
518 Servicios Profesionales y Tecnicos, S.A.
519 Ideal, Inc.
520 Adriana Gil/Alta Cocina
521 Restaurante
522 Restaurante Bar

523

524

525

526

527

528

529

530

523 K.D. Modular Furniture System
524 Diprec, S.A.
525 Mediterranee
526 Banamex, S.A.
527 Trak, S.A.
528 Grill de Puebla/Hoteles Mision, S.A.
529 Ancla, S.A.
530 Telart, S.A.

531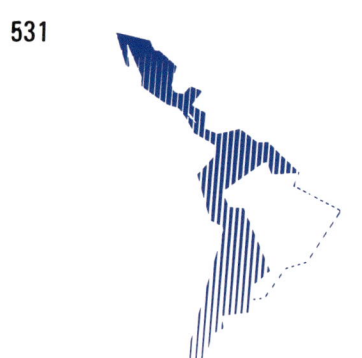

532

533

534 la torre

535

536

537
Sta. Maria del Obraje

538

531  IBM de Mexico, S.A.
532  Le Fromage, S.A. de C.V.
533  Ideal, Inc.
534  Distribuidora La Torre, S.A.
535  Grupo Quetzal Club/Discoteque
536  Operadora de Equipos Maritmos, S.A. de C.V.
537  Desarrollo Turistico
538  Patricia Quintana/Alta Cocina

**539**

**540**

**541**

**542**

**543**

**544**

**545**

**546**

539  Presidencia
540  Grupo Primex
541  Royal Care Services
542  Hoteles Oasis Internacional
543  Inmobiliaria Turistica Muella, S.A.
544  Hoteles Mision, S.A.
545  The Crab
546  Restaurant

547

548

549

550

551

552

553

CARIBE PLAZA

554

555

547 Grupo Todos, S.A. de C.V.
548 Grupo LBC, S.C. Arquitectos
549 Opequimar, S.A.
550 Restaurant
551 Realtor, S.A. de C.V.
552 Invermonedas
553 Dipro/Diseno y Produccion Creativa, S.A. de C.V.
554 Banco Nacional de Mexico, S.N.C./Cuenta Maestra
555 Diseno e Iluminacion Lamda, S.A. de C.V.

**Richard Muller**
West Germany
556-559

556 Einkaufscenter
557 Messebau Wirtz
558 Getrankegrosshandel
559 Kurhotel am Kaiserbrunnen

**Rolf Ruiz**
Port of Spain, Trinidad
560-563

560

561

562

563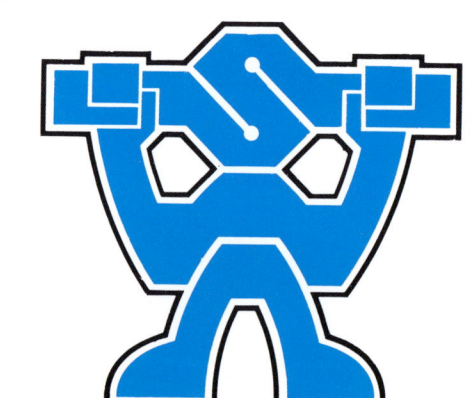

560 Jones Animal Clinic and Hospital
561 Arnold's Pastry & Pizza
562 Bergerac Furniture Showrooms
563 Steel Workers Association of Trinidad and Tobago

**Kan Tai-keung Design & Assocs.**
Wanchai, Hong Kong
564-569

564

565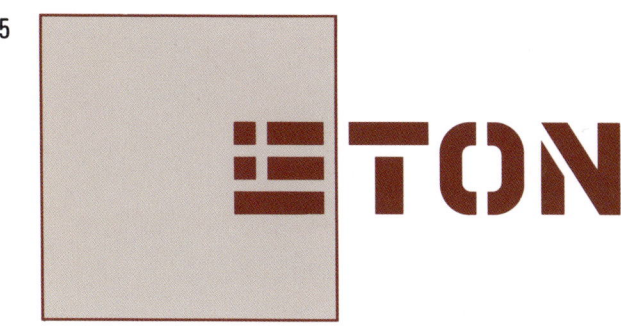

566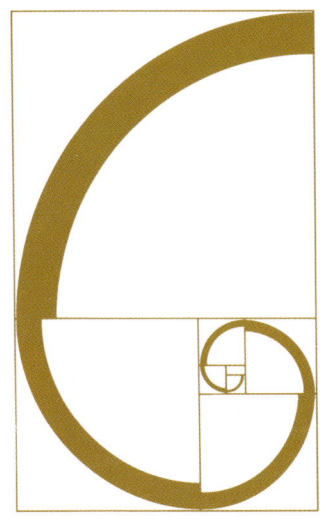

567
城市画廊 City Gallery

568

569   east east wonton

564 Lutex Company Limited
565 Eton Properties Limited
566 Cheung-Macpherson & Co., Ltd.
567 City Gallery
568 GP Wedding Service Centre Ltd.
569 YHY Food Products Limited

**Pentti Ruuska**
Vantaa Finland
570–575

570

571

572

573

574

575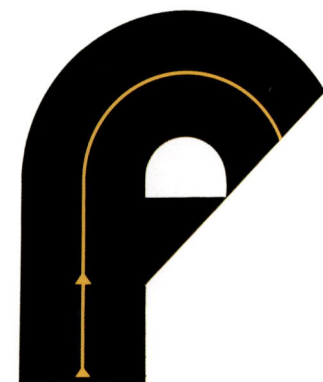

570 Arts Exhibition
571 Catering Suppliers
572 Gourmet Department
573 Folk Music Festival
574 Accordian Folk Music Group
575 Foto Sokos

**Armin Vogt Partner**
Graphic Design SGV ASG
Basel, Switzerland
**576–585**

576 PARAFON

577 CHAMAeLEON

578

579

580

581

582

583

584

585

576 Cilag AG
577 Chamaeleon Verlag AG
578 Edwin Vogt Partner AG
579 Basler Grafiker
580 Hasena AG
581 Balair AG
582 Chamaeleon Verlag AG
583 Cilag AG
584 Fiat Italia
585 Cilag AG

**Formata**
Mexico
586-604

586

587

588    589    590

591

592

586 Jardin Guadalupano, S.A.
587 Grupo Industrial N.K.S., S.A. DE C.V.
588 TRV, Ltd.
589 Manufacturas Electricas, S.A.
590 Plaza Emarcadero
591 Rati Trap
592 Pronatura Asociacion Mexicana Pro Conservacion De La Naturaleza

593

594

595

596 
anso administraciones s.a.

597

598

599 
LOBBY JARDIN

600

593 Procesadora Lovimex, S.A.
594 Grupo Saproc
595 Barragan Jimenez Y Loperena
596 Anso Administraciones, S.A.
597 Herramientas Grupo Mochis, S.A.
598 Electronica Steren, S.A.
599 Lobby Jardin
600 Teca-Caoba-Ceiba Condominium

601

602

603

604

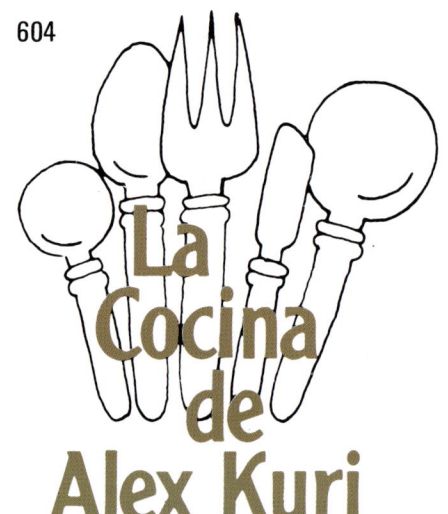

601 Multibanco Mercantil De Mexico, S.A.
602 Carton Fenix, S.A.
603 Industrias Cretarve, S.A. DE C.V.
604 La Cocina De Alex Kuri

**Guillermo Gonzalez Ruiz**
Buenos Aires, Argentina
605-619

605

606

607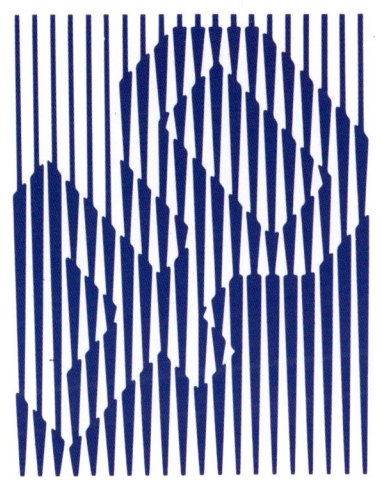

608

609

610

611

605 "Consejo Publicitario"
606 "Antorhas Foundation"
607 40th Anniversary "Clarin" Journal
608 "Universidad De Buenos Aires, Siglo XXI" (UBAXXI)
609 "Clubttipico Parque Burnett"
610 Banco de Tuerra Del Fuego
611 Ferragen

612

613

614

615

616

617

618

619

612 "Dorotea Oliva"
613 Gatopardo
614 "Canos Y Accesorios"
615 "Las Tejas"
616 "Gatopardo"
617 Roland Cotton
618 Tobra
619 Telebanco

Young-Jae Cho
Korea
620-633

620

621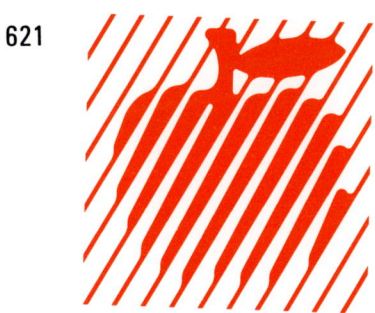

622

623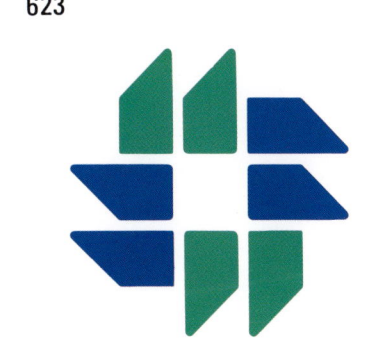

624

625

626

620 The Citizens National Bank
621 Dongsuh Foods Corp.
622 Samlip Foods Industrial Co., Ltd.
623 Korea Exchange Bank
624 Chungbuk Bank
625 Dong—A Pharmaceutical Co., Ltd.
626 Daehankyoyuk Life Insurance Co., Ltd.

627

628

629

630

631

632

633

627 Kia Motors Corp.
628 Daelim Industrial Co., Ltd.
629 Riverside Hotel Seoul
630 Shinsegae Department Store Co., Ltd.
631 Korea Investment Trust Co., Ltd.
632 Peeres Cosmetics, Ltd.
633 Korea Merchant Banking Corp.

**McManus & Associates Limited**
Toronto, Ontario, Canada
634-650

634 Postmark Toronto
635 McManus & Associates
636 The Grand Spectacle
637 Marathon Brown

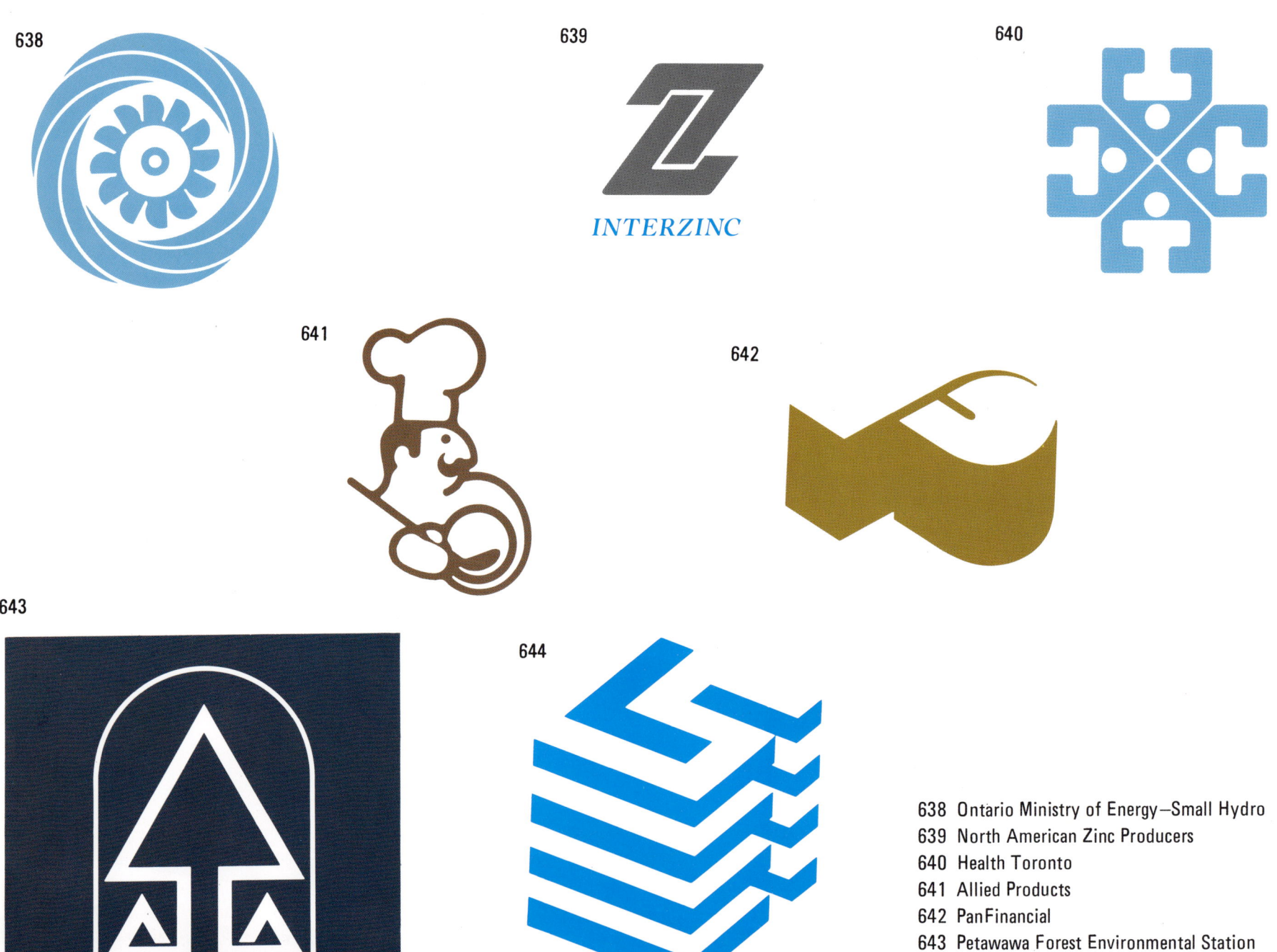

638 Ontario Ministry of Energy—Small Hydro
639 North American Zinc Producers
640 Health Toronto
641 Allied Products
642 PanFinancial
643 Petawawa Forest Environmental Station
644 Leader Structures

645  Yabu Pushelberg
646  Nature Conservancy of Canada
647  Accents
648  A Securities Broker
649  Cosma
650  Stafford Motion

**Angelo Sganzerla**
Milano, Italy
**651-660**

651

652

653

654

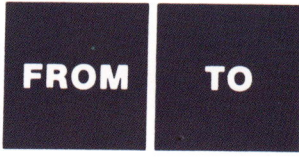

655

651 Marizibill
652 Gli Orsolini
653 Studio III
654 FROM TO srl
655 Proposte

**656** PICOWA

**657** AMARANTA

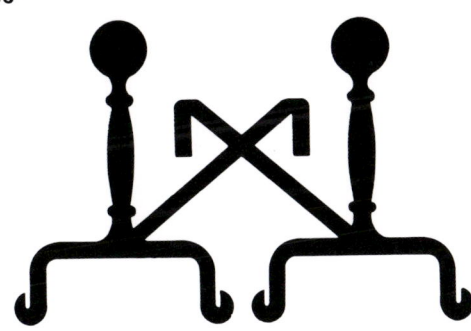

656 Picowa srl
657 Amaranta srl
658 Il Lichene Edizioni
659 Studio Besana
660 Mario Monti

**Ricardo Rey Studio Inc.**
Puerto Rico
661-690

661

662

663

664

665

666

661 Bodegas Argentinas Corp.
662 Cultured, Inc. (Washington)
663 UNI-Serv., Inc.
664 Salones Don Quijote
665 La Tasca Del Callejon
666 Fersan

667

668

669

670

671

672

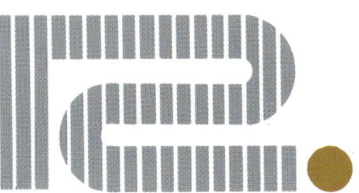

673

674

667 V.I.P. Security Systems Corp.
668 Elite Corporation
669 Carimar Corp. (Miami)
670 14K Gold (Mayaquez)
671 Deli, Restaurant Argentino
672 Poseidon Corporation
673 Mail Center
674 Shampoo Salon

675 Joyeria Universal Inc.
676 Chevres Enterprises Inc.
677 ADCO
678 Special Productions
679 EL Mall
680 Tiendas La Tijera
681 El Paseo Restaurant
682 Langostinos Del Caribe

683

684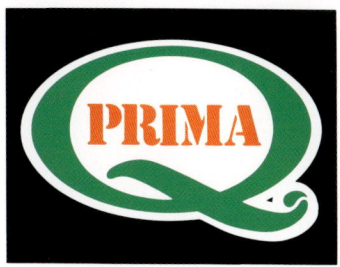

685

686

687

688

689

690

683 Suit City
684 Prima Quality Farms, Inc.
685 Relojes Y Relojes
686 Continental Shipping Inc.
687 Ristorante Fontana Di Roma
688 Verticales Y Mas
689 Siembra
690 Los Chavales Restaurant

**Vlad Mosmondor**
Canberra Australia
**691-770**

691

692

693

694

695

696

697

691 National Capital Development Commission
692 Adventure Workshop in Innovation and Entrepreneurship
693 Technology Transfer Council
694 Hawker College
695 Forth International Plant Pathology Congress Melbourne
696 Clay Target Shooting Association ACT
697 Canberra Festival

698

699

700
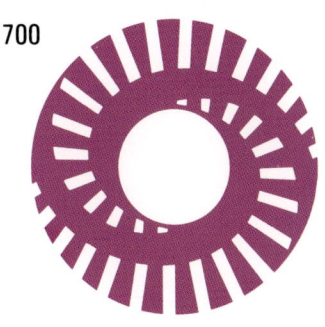

701

702

703

704

705

698  Construct Design Research Unit
699  Pay Parking
700  Information Technology Council
701  Pavefill
702  Australian National Sport Centre Canberra
703  Dan and Dan Forestry Services
704  A F N W
705  National Bushfire Research Unit CSIRO

706

707

708

709

710

711

712

713

706 Neilson Associates
707 Data Conversion Corporation Pty. Ltd.
708 BHP Science Price
709 Canberra Theatre Centre
710 Bruce College TAFE
711 Auslang Australian Supply Language
712 Southern Tree Breeding Association Inc.
713 Cangraphics Pty. Ltd.

714

715

716

717

718

719

720

721

714 Canberra Country Club
715 Atelje 28
716 Forest Research CSIRO
717 Confederation of ACT Industry
718 Canberra Public Library Service
719 Farrer Pharmacy
720 Tempo Theatre
721 Canberra City Centre

722

723

724

725

726

727

728

729

722 Graham Osborne and Associates
723 Yaffa K Richard
724 Yarralumla Soft
725 Australian Curriculum Development Centre
726 U Spit
727 Lee Pratt Pty Ltd.
728 CINCH
729 DECOIN

730

731

732

733

734

735

736

737

730 BBYG
731 Canberra Art Teachers Association
732 Donnan Transport Pty. Ltd.
733 Hudine Canberra Tents
734 ACROD
735 Monographics
736 CMW
737 Cangraphics Data Systems Pty. Ltd.

738

739

740
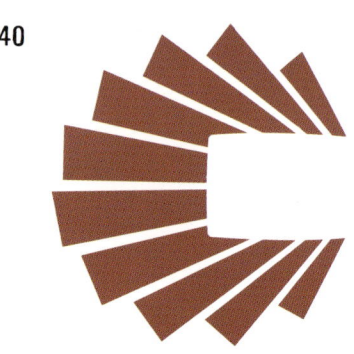

741

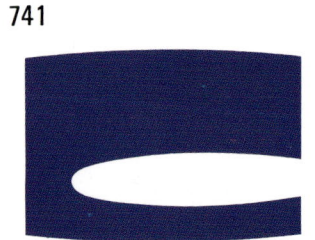

742

743

744

745

738 Australian Year of the Tree ACT
739 SOS Fyshwich Commercial Centre
740 National Information Technology Council Inc.
741 Cangraphics Pty. Ltd.
742 Airship Enterprises
743 Model City
744 Curtin Primary School
745 GraphCard Aid

746 growtrees

747

748

749

750

751

752

753

746 Growtrees
747 Billabong Recreation Centre Tuggeranong
748 BOMA
749 ANZIF
750 Australian Space Office
751 Catholic Social Services
752 Ministry of Family Development
753 Holy Family Gourie

754
755
756

757
758
759
760

761
762

754 Catholic Education Office
755 St. Peter Chanel Yarralumla
756 Croation Social Welfare
757 Geoffrey F. Mayne Catholic Military Prelate
758 Bishop Patrick Power
759 Archbishop of Sydney Edward Bede Clancy
760 Archbishop of Canberra and Goulburn
761 St. Raphael's Parish Queanbeyan
762 St. Christopher Cathedral Canberra

763

764

765

766

767

768

769

770

763 Catholic Military Prelature of Australia
764 Archdiocies of Broken Bay
765 Patrick Laurence Murphy Bishop of Broken Bay
766 Patrick Laurence Murphy Bishop of Broken Bay
767 Patrick Laurence Murphy Bishop of Broken Bay
768 Catholic Church Development Fund
769 The Sixth Assembly of the World Council of Churches
770 Southern Cross

**Terry O Communications Inc.**
Canada
**771-773**

771

772

773

771 International Fish Packers Co. Ltd.
772 Fong & Fong Holdings Ltd.
773 Interlink

**Dionisio Petrelli/Diseno Grafico**
Caracas
774-791

774

775

776

777

778

779

774 Jose Antonio De La Guerra y De La Paz
775 Marco Polo
776 Il Foro Romano
777 Eavox
778 Inforven 86
779 Weekends

780

781

782

783

784

785

780  Tecnica Moore
781  Capital Express
782  Madison
783  Sistemas Logitron C.A.
784  Supermarket
785  Supermarket 2

786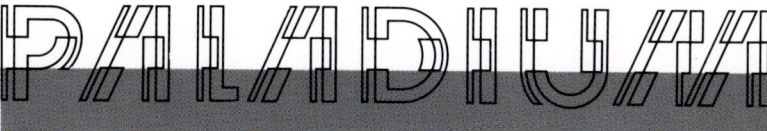

787

788

789

790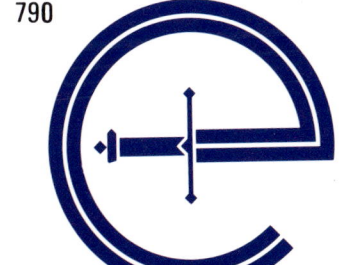

791

786 Paladium
787 Epson Rent
788 Aurora
789 Xenon
790 Excalibur
791 30 Comercial Nunez

**Telmet Design Associates**
Canada
**792-798**

792 Raintree Development Corporation Limited
793 Webcom Limited
794 Richman Group
795 FRC Composites Limited
796 Caruba Holdings Limited
797 Charterhouse Equities Limited
798 Women's Business Development Centre

**Dicken Castro & Cia**
Bogota
**799-822**

799

800

801

802

803

804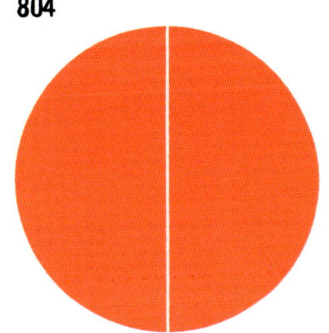

805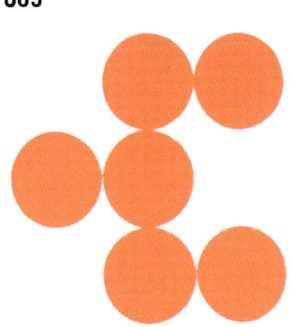

799 Colcurtidos
800 Cementos Diamante
801 Grupo Social
802 Ecominas
803 Tableros De Colombia
804 Movimiento Familiar Colombiano
805 Compensar

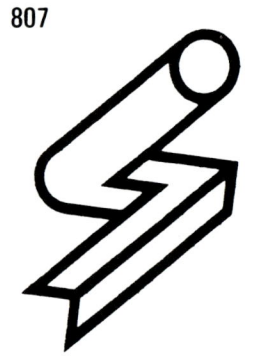
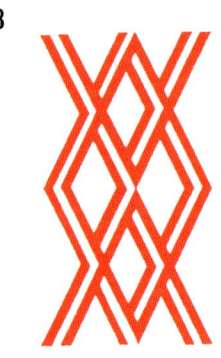

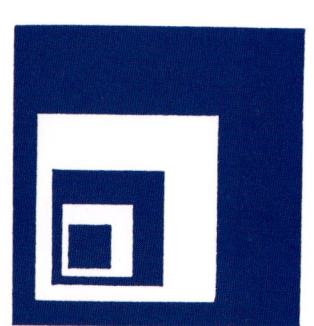

806 Tecnicana
807 Siderurgica De Boyaca
808 40 Anos Sociedad Colombiana De Arquitectos
809 Colombian Bags
810 Anuario De Arquitectura
811 Centro De Arte Actual
812 Grupo Prometeo
813 Ospinas Y CIA

814

GRC

815

816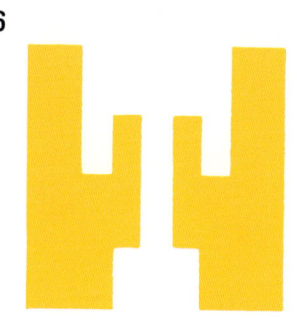

817

818

819

820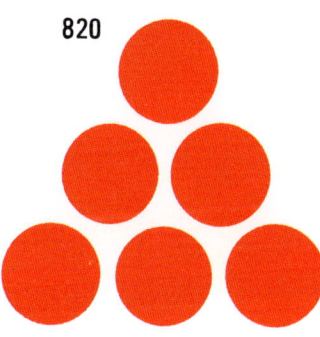

821

822

814 Grupo Radial Colombiano
815 Comunbana Panama
816 La Tertulia
817 Organizacion Luis Carlos Sarmiento Angulo
818 Cofinatura
819 Banco Del Estado
820 Escuela De Administracion Publica
821 Instituto Roosevelt Colombia
822 Omnes

**Morteza Momayez**
Iran
823-830

823

824

825

826

823 Elmi Poblishing Co.
824 Faculty of Medical Science
825 Omour Cinemaie Film Prod.
826 Ghoba, Aid Social Center

827

828

829

830

827 Iramo Belgium Trading Co.
828 Design Study for a Cultural Center
829 Ayandeh
830 Aid Social Center

**Bryce Design**
Australia
831-853

831

832

833

834

835

836

837

831 John Walsh Architects Pty. Ltd.
832 The Royal Australian Institute of Architects
833 Gordon Pacific Limited
834 Kirkegard Architects
835 Henderson Trout Solicitors and Notaries
836 Art Gallery of New South Wales
837 Sydney Cove Authority

838

839

840

841

842

843

844

845

838 Riverside Centre, Lend Lease
839 Queensland Conservation of Music
840 Anderson Street Architects
841 Caroma
842 Oilmin
843 Australian War Memorial
844 Australian Council of National Trusts
845 Paradise Centre, H.S.P. Nominees Ltd.

846

847

848

849

850

851

852

853

846 Raptis Plaza, Raptis Developments
847 The Lyrebird Restaurant
848 75th Anniversary of Royal Australian Navy
849 Caves Beach Resort
850 Hyatt Regency Coolum Resort
851 Bond University
852 Brisbane Community Arts Centre
853 Esk Shire Council

**Ron Ellis Designs Trademarks**
England
**854-889**

854

855

856

857

858

854  Jack/Tully
855  Grenfell-Baines Award Building Design Partnership
856  Entertainment Installations
857  Bristol United Press Evening & Morning Papers
858  Retail Hi-Fi

859

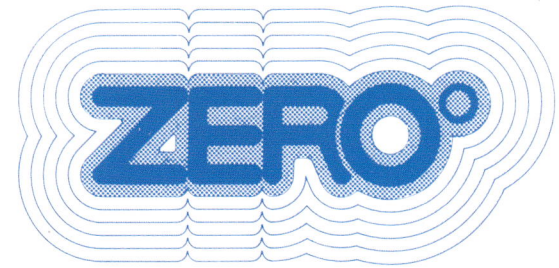

860

861

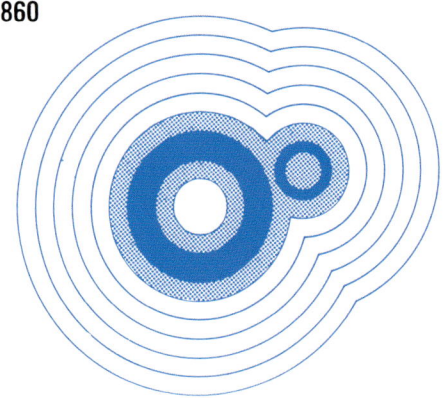

862

863

864

865

866

859 ZERO Freezer Food
860 ZERO Freezer Food
861 Mobile Disco
862 Rosemary/Abrahams
863 Temporary Office Personnel Services
864 ARABUILD United Arab Emirates
865 Meon Valley
866 South Marston Country Club

867

868

869

870

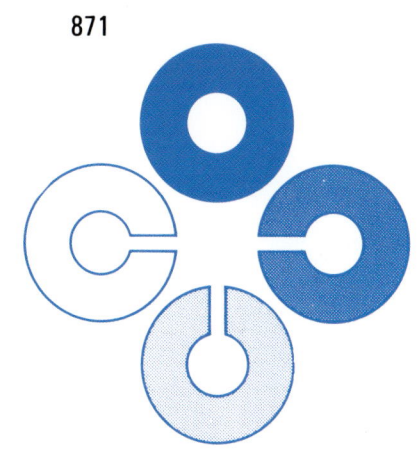
871

872

873

874

867 Alleycat Female Boutique
868 Corimport
869 Guy Male Boutique
870 Six Ways Sports
871 Clockwork Office Cleaning Company
872 Aquarius
873 Great Yarmouth Warehousing Company
874 Centenary, The Royal National Rose Society

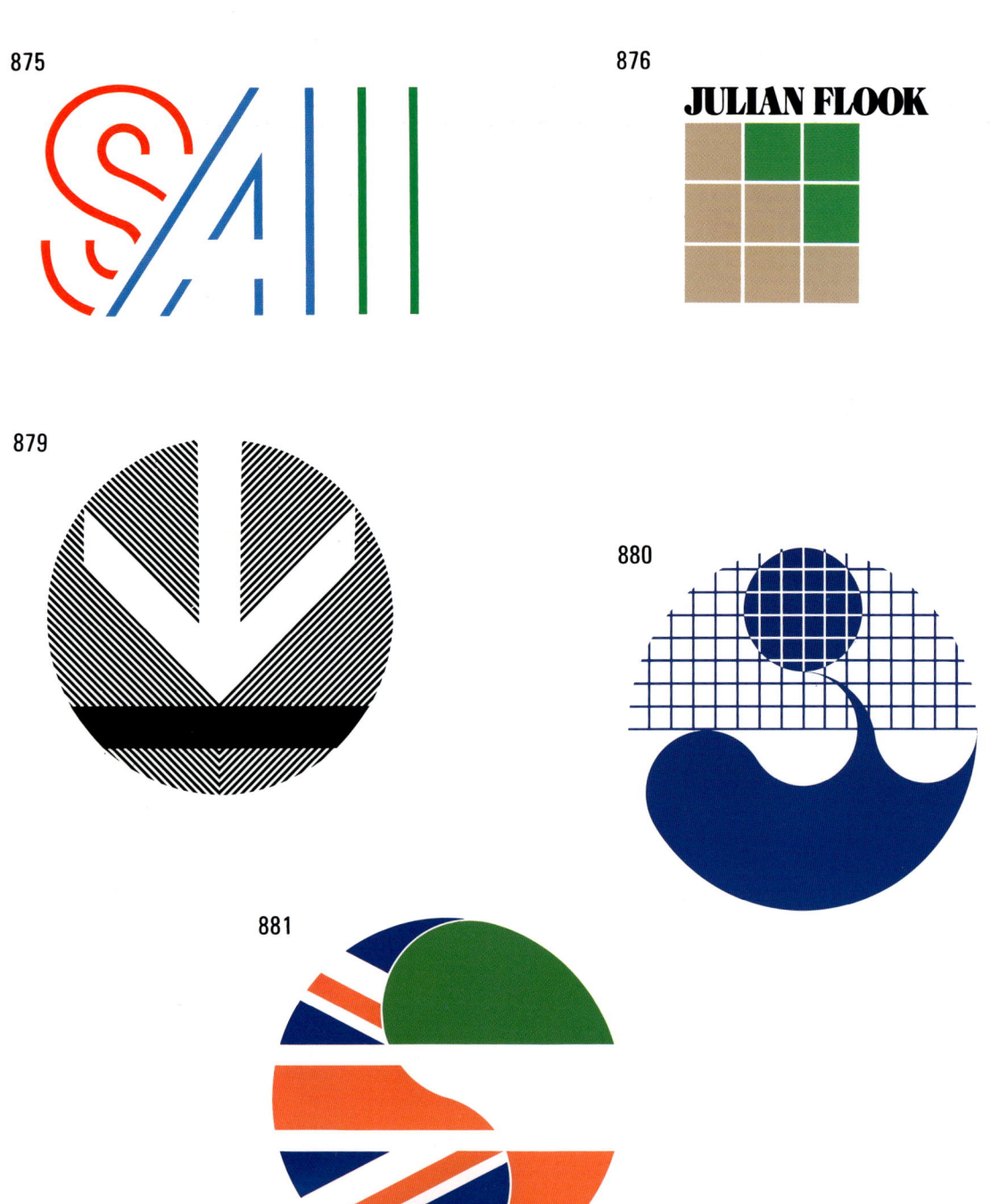

875 The Society of Architectural Illustrators
876 Julian Flook
877 Supermarkets
878 Wineshops
879 M & R Flooring
880 Ashton Court Country Club
881 Interact UK/IRAN

882

883

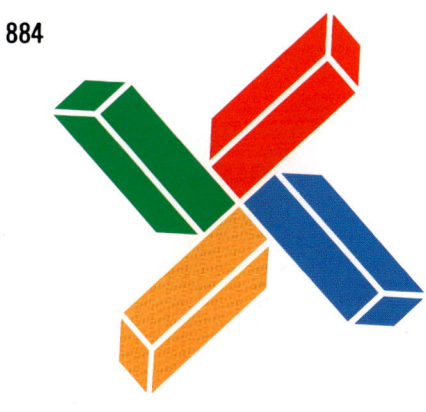
884

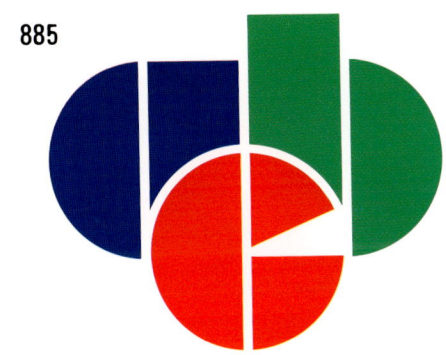
885

886

887

888

889

882 Vincent & Jerrom
883 Landel
884 Bricks & Building Supplies Ltd.
885 Avon Business Centre
886 Family Life
887 Outlines Landscape Consultants
888 IDC, International Design & Construction
889 Universal Signs

**Kan Tai-Keung**
Wanchai, Hong Kong
**890-893**

890 Sea Swallow Tissue Paper
891 Regent Restaurant
892 Product Safety Exhibition
893 SS Design & Production

**Michael Herold**
Germany
894-943

894

895

894 Das Emblem "modernes Buro" erganzt durch Mitfuhrung der Jahreszahl

895 Das Zeichen CMT wird erst durch die Jahreszahl Komplett

**896**

**897**

**898**

**899**

**900**
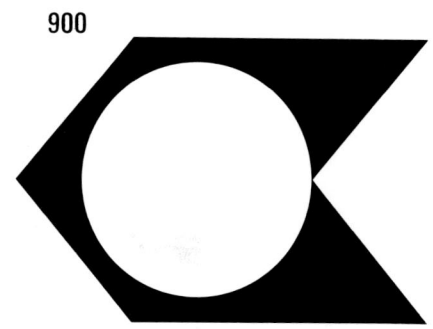

**901**
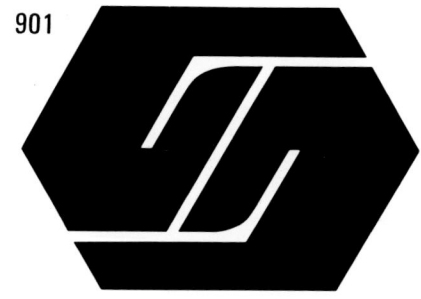

**902**

**903**

896 Atelier Agethen
897 Signet der Verbraucherausstellung FAMIA
898 Westmeisterschaften der Friseure
899 Bundesfachschau fur das Hotelgewerbe
900 Internationale Waffenborse
901 Zeichen der INTERHOSPITAL und FAB
902 Informationsschau UMELT 72
903 Garten Ausstellurg

904

905

906

907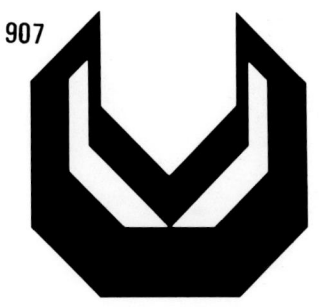

908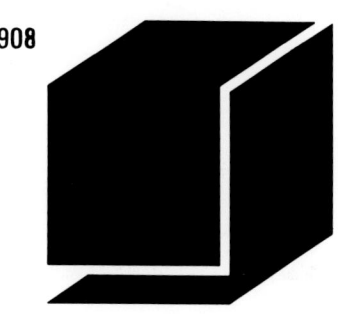

909

910

911

904 Ausstellung fur Medizen-Technik
905 SUDBACK
906 Zeichenfurden Hohenpark Killesberg
907 Fachausstellung fur Heimwerkerbedarf DIY
908 Fachausstellung fur Raumausstatter
909 Internationale Sammlerborse
910 das moderne buro
911 Fachausstellung Metall

912

913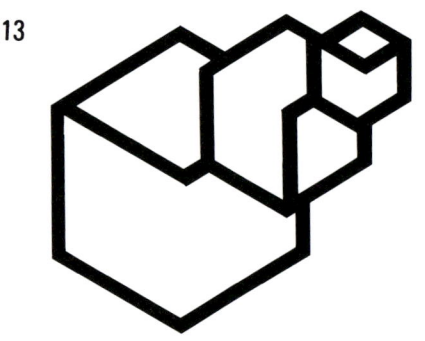

914

915

916

917

918

919

912 CLUB
913 Holzmann & Hosmann Blitzschutzanlagen
914 Verkaufsausstellung Antiquitaten
915 Fortbildungskongress der Arzte
916 Informationsfachschau ENERGIE NACH MASS
917 Gas und Wasserversorgung
918 Lutz Feufel
919 Landesstelle fur Betriebsschutz

920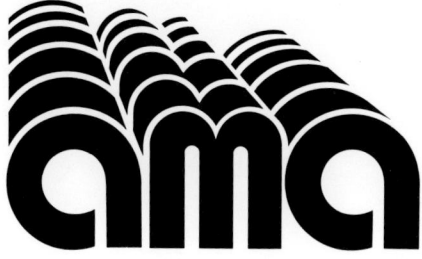
921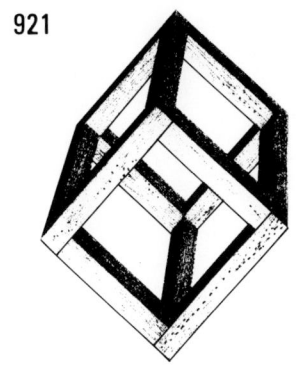
922
923
924
925
926
927

920 Auto-und Motorrad-Ausstellung
921 Holzverarbeitung Fachausstellung
922 Ausstellung Computer im Handwerk
923 HIFI
924 Euroschau
925 Fliesenleger Koch
926 Suddeutsche Fachmesse fur das Fleischerhandwerk
927 Arztekongress

928

929

930

931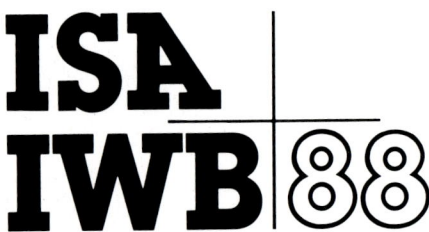

932

933

934

935

928 Ultra Bauzentrum
929 Sonderschau Seegarten
930 Ausstellung und Festival Jugend 2000
931 ISA & IWB – Int. Sammlerborse, Int. Waffenborse
932 Fachausstellung HOBBY ELEKTRONIK
933 PRO SANITA – Fachausstellung fur Gesundheit und Natur
934 Schleyer-Halle Stuttgart
935 Ausstellung Handwerk

936

937

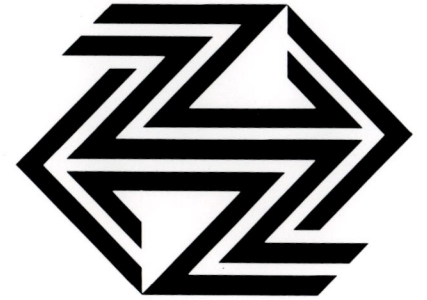

938

939

940

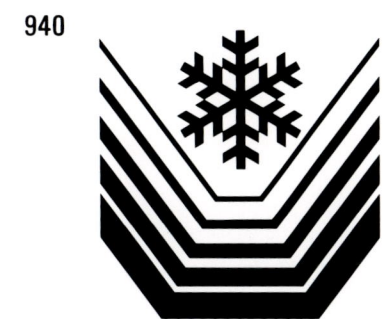

941

942

943

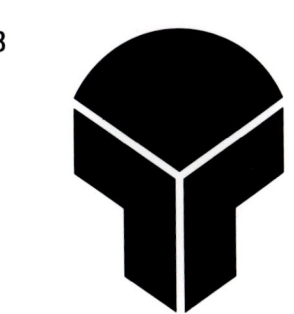

936 Ausstellung der Kunst
937 EL TEFA
938 AMB-Ausstellung fur Metallbearbeitung
939 Theissen Bauzentrale
940 Ausstellung fur Winter-Tourismus
941 Signet der Messe Stuttgart
942 Autosalon Stuttgart
943 INNOTEK

**Total Design bv**
Amsterdam
**944-949**

944

945

946

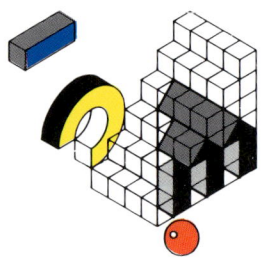

947

948

949

944 Pallas & Basys Combinatie
945 Y-Tech
946 Macobouw
947 Koninklijk Instituut voor de Tropen
948 Onderwijs en Wetenschappen
949 Nederlandse Orde van Accountants-
    Administratieconsulenten

**BON**
Italy
**950-991**

950

951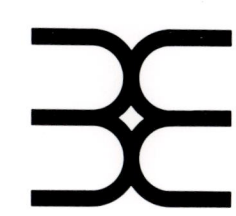

952

953

954

955

956

950 Impianti Industriali
951 Orologi
952 Alberghi
953 Infanzia
954 Tipolitografia
955 Automobili
956 Vini

957
958
959

960
961
962

963
964

957 Rheoplastici
958 Officine Meccaniche
959 Prodotti per Capelli
960 Supermercati
961 Costruzioni
962 Convegno
963 Piattaforme Aeree
964 Import

965
966
967

968
969
970
971

972
973

965 Bigiotteria
966 Meccanica
967 Imbottiti
968 Ittici
969 Albergo
970 Ass. Tecnici Cemento
971 Servizi Aziendali
972 Costruzioni Telefoniche
973 Perle

974

975

976

977

978

974 Camere Commercia Estero Veneto
975 Costruzioni
976 Catering
977 Edizioni Fotografiche
978 Automobili

979 [NELI logo]

980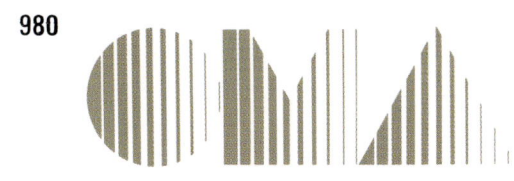

981 B!COLOR

982

983

984

979 Abbigliamento Femminile
980 Lampade Illuminazione
981 Colorificio
982 Acquedotto Venezia
983 Legno: progettazione e ricerca
984 Servizi Aziendali

985

986

987

*millepiedi*

988

989

990

985 Ruote in Lega
986 Caravan
987 Calzature
988 Lame-dischi da taglio
989 Edizioni
990 Calzature Sportive

991 Simboli grafici realizzati per un Periodico di Annunci Economici

**Jorge Canales/Consultores Creative**
Cuauhtemos No. 69 Coyoacan
04000 Mexico, D.F.
**992-996**

992  Muebles de Cuernavaca Morelos, S.A.
993  Instituto Mexicano del Seguró Social
994  Valores Mexicanos S.A. Casa de bolsa
995  Valores Mexicanos. Fondo de inversion.
996  Bachoco/Design Associates

**Diana Garcia de Tolone**
Edo. de Mexico
997-1000

997

998

999

1000

997 CIA. Nestle S.A.
998 Danone De Mexico S.A.
999 CIA. Nestle S.A.
1000 Almidones Mexicanos S.A.

**Kenneth Hollick FSIAD**
Blackheath, London
**1001-1004**

1001

1002

1003

SEAS●NS

1004

1001 Associated Independent Stores
1002 Associated Independent Stores
1003 Seasons
1004 Country Bunches

**Alfonso Garcia Reyes/Paloma Ibanes**
Disenadores Y Consultores
**1005-1007**

1005

1006

1007

1005 Campestre Restaurant
1006 Dentist Gloria Garcia
1007 Camara De Comercio De Gustavo A. Madero

Erno Sara
Hungary-Europe
1008-1013

1008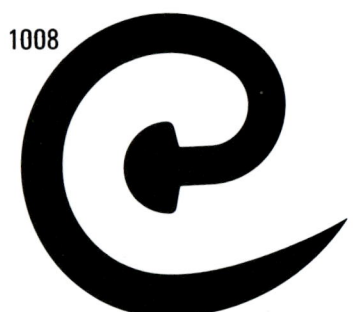

1009

1010

1011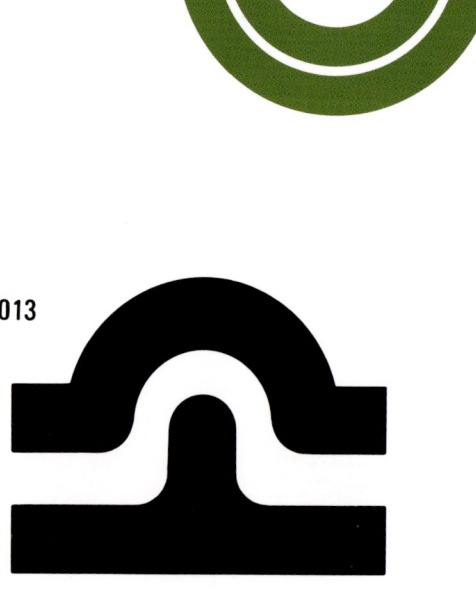

1012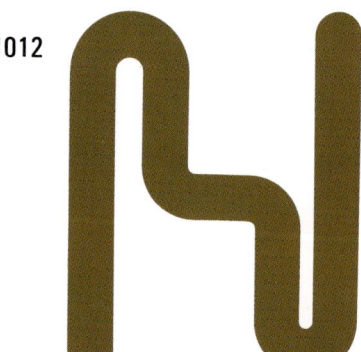

1013

1008 Ezermester Bolt
1009 Magyar Hirdeto
1010 Best Poster of Year Exibition
1011 Oktangep
1012 Hindermann Sitzmobel
1013 Planeterium-Budapest

**Arq. Andres Garcia Paz**
Diseno Y Comunicacion, S.A.
Juarez, Edo. de Mexico
**1014-1032**

1014

1015

1016

1017

1018

1019

1014 Capitan Nemo's Diving Club
1015 Grupo Corydora
1016 Diseno Garcia Paz
1017 Pasteleria "La Abeja"
1018 Promocional
1019 Empacadora De Alimentos

1020
1021
1022
1023
1024
1025
1026

1020 Telematica De Mexico
1021 Promociones Financieras
1022 Grupo Sidura, S.A. DE C.V.
1023 Productos Inhibidores Del Fuego, S.A.
1024 C.W. Johnson
1025 Actimoda
1026 Grupo Kaltex

**1027**

**1028**

**1029**

**1030**

**1031**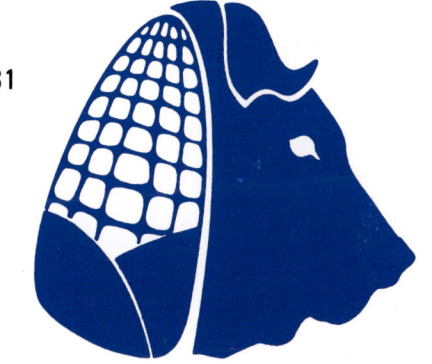

**1032**

1027 International Finance Club
1028 Diseno Y Comunicacion
1029 Promociones Financieras
1030 Promocional
1031 Agricola Logo
1032 Agencia Aduanal Luis Hoyo

**WM de MAJO**
London, England
**1033-1043**

1033

1034

1035

1036

1033 John Millar & Sons
1034 Unicom Ltd.
1035 Ti-Well Ltd.
1036 Printwell Ltd.

1037

*Letts* of London®

1038

1039

1040

1042

1041

1043

1037 Letts Script Logo
1038 Letts "L" Symbol
1039 Letts Script Logo
1040 Letts Script Logo
1041 Letts Link Logo
1042 Powell Ltd.
1043 Bi-Rite Ltd.

**David Consuegra**
Bogota 2, Colombia
1044-1120

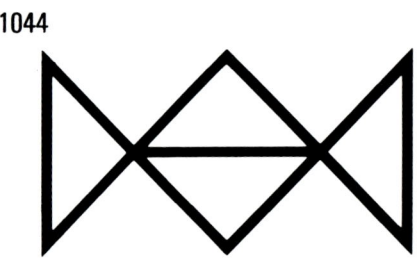
1044

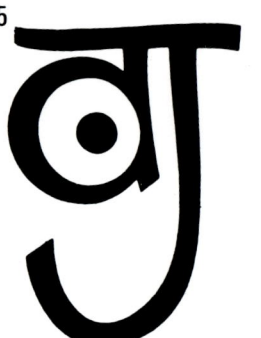
1045

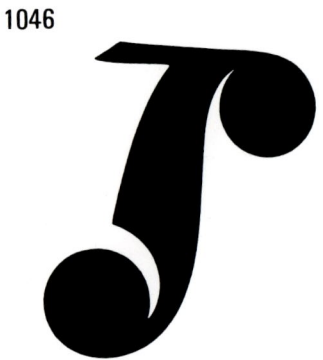
1046

1047

1048

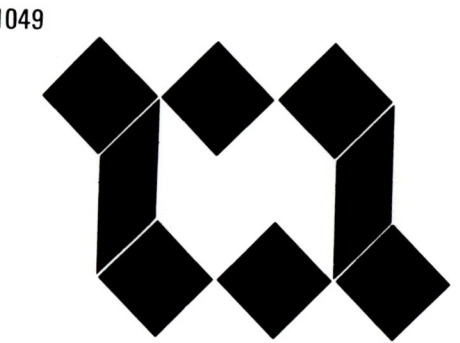
1049

1050

1051

1044 Museo de Arte Moderno de Bogota
1045 John Awtrey
1046 John Strail
1047 Teatro La Mama
1048 Escuela Nacional de Arquitectura
1049 Reinaldo Arenas
1050 Centro Planeacion y Urbanismo
1051 Escuela de Arquitectura

1052
1053
1054
1055
1056
1057
1058
1059

1052 Campana Nacional de Limpieza Bucal
1053 Primer Festival Atletico Internacional
1054 Mercedes Mosquera
1055 Coro Univeristario
1056 II Festival de Teatro de Camara
1057 Libreria Contemporanea
1058 Premio Esso de Novela
1059 Abdu Eljaiek

1060
1061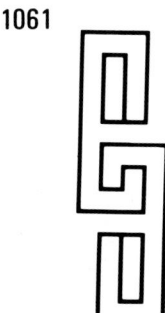
1062
1063 
1064
1065
1066
1067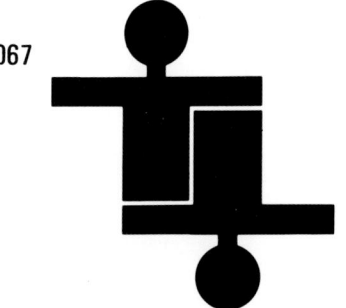

1060 Rosemarie Schlenker
1061 Escuela de Artes
1062 Petroquimicas del Atlantico
1063 San Jorge
1064 Editorial Horizontes
1065 Ediciones Testimonio
1066 Inravision
1067 Terapia Fisca y Psiquica

1068

1069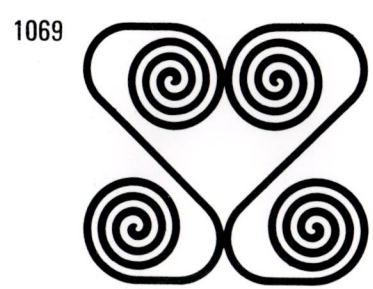

1070

1071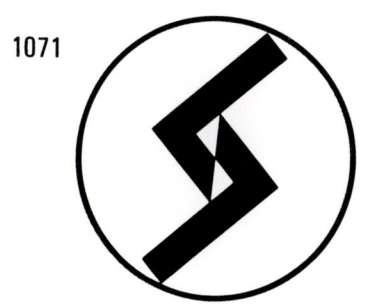

1072

1073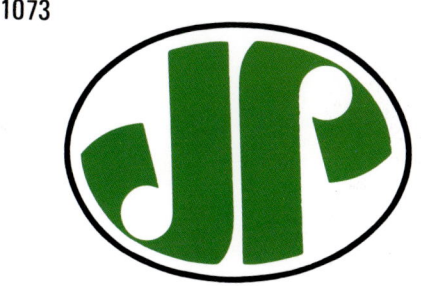

1074

1075

1068 Camara de Comerico de Bucaramanga
1069 Sono Zeta
1070 Producciones Graficas
1071 Loteria de Santander
1072 Libreria Iris
1073 J. Plata Cia. Ltda.
1074 Cigarros Hugo
1075 Maquinaq

1076

1077

1078

1079

1080

1081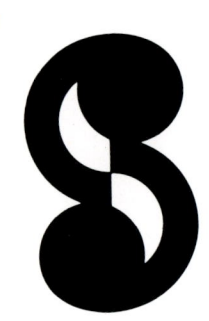

1082

1083

1076 Curtidivi
1077 Constancia
1078 Editorial Vanguardia
1079 Luis Lloreda
1080 Aceace
1081 Corporacion Financiera de Santander
1082 Marianda
1083 Artesanias de Colombia S.A.

 1084
 1085
 1086
 1087
 1088
 1089
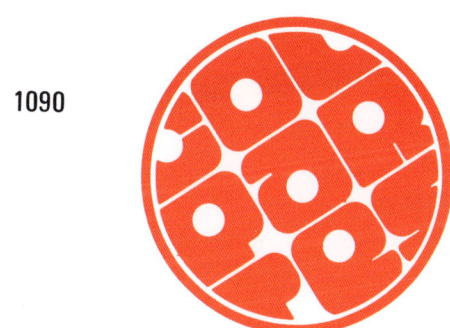 1090
 1091

1084 Logia de Los Andes
1085 Casajan
1086 Empresas Publicas de Bucaramanga
1087 Textilgrupo
1088 Prodac
1089 Polyplas
1090 Colpartes
1091 Biblioteca Publica Municipal Gabriel Turbay

1092
1093
1094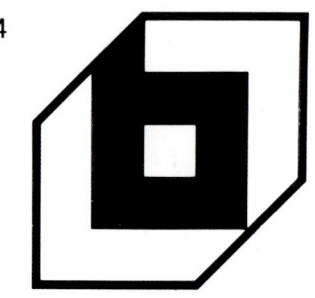
1095
1096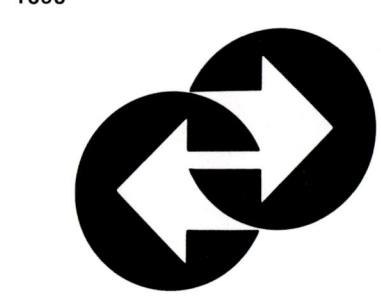
1097
1098
1099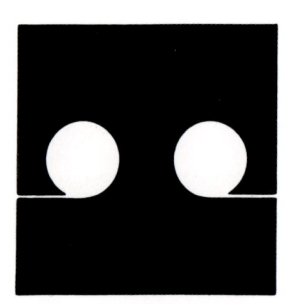

1092 Universidad Industrial de Santader
1093 Centro de Rehabiltacion Infantil San Juan Bautista
1094 Bienes Culturales
1095 Corporacion Forestal de Santander
1096 Centro Comercial Rosedal
1097 Incap Ltda.
1098 Asociacion Santandereana de Optometras
1099 Tretalce

1100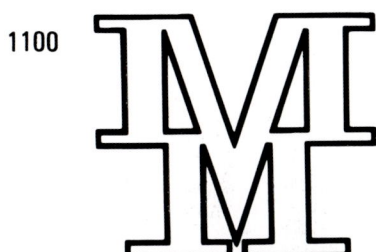
1101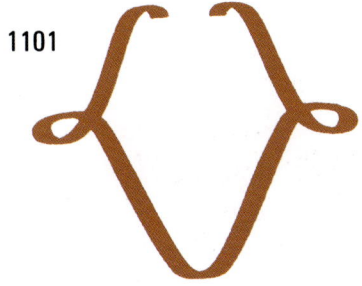
1102
1103
1104
1105
1106
1107

1100 Maximas Minimas
1101 Loma Verde
1102 Mauricia Angel
1103 Corbanca
1104 Taller de Giangrandi
1105 Croydon S.A.
1106 Facultad de Artes
1107 Avidesa

1108

1109

1110

1111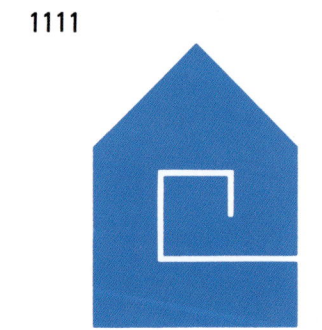

1112

1113

1114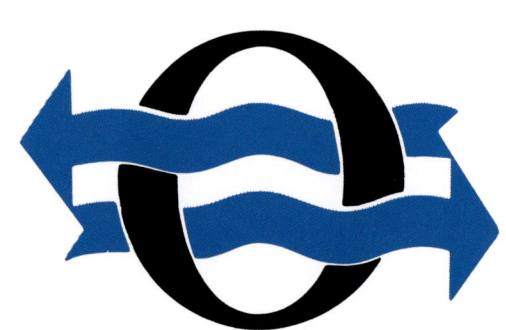

1115

1108 Fondo Cultural Cafetero
1109 Marabu
1110 Conseguridad
1111 Conadi LTDA.
1112 Siluetas
1113 Congregacion de Jesus y Maria
1114 Overseas Contract Services
1115 Damas Rosadas

1116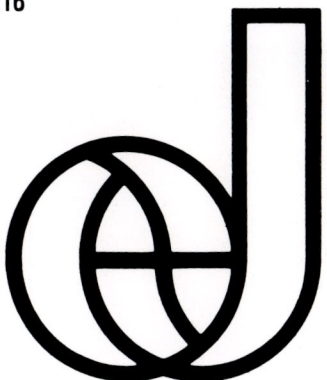

1117

1118

1119

1120

1116 Emisora Javeriana
1117 Cifi
1118 Sandri
1119 Instituto Nacional de Cancerologia
1120 CID

**Rogerio Martins**
Rio De Janeiro, Brasil
**1121-1179**

1121

1122

1123

1124

1125

1126

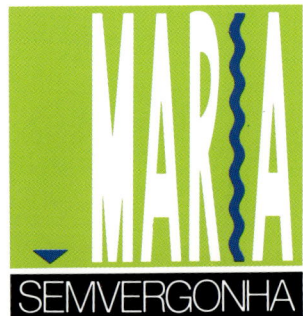

1121 Taormina
1122 Redley
1123 Redley
1124 Briho
1125 Casa Da Foto
1126 Maria Sem Vergonha

1127

1128

1129
CONPLAN
CONSULTORIA
PROJETOS &
PLANEJAMENTO
EMPRESARIAL

1130
GELI
MOREIRA
DE SOUZA
DECORAÇÕES

1131

1132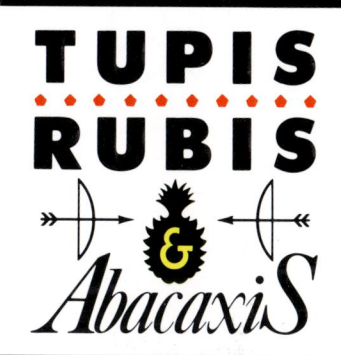

1133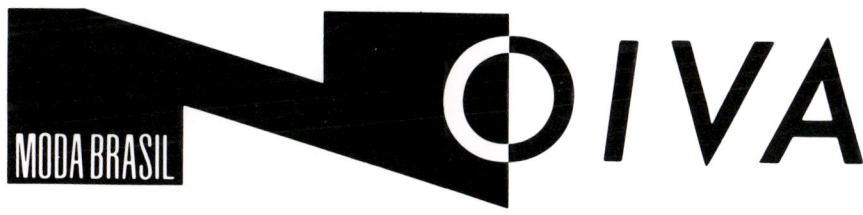

1127 Cantao
1128 Expedition Company
1129 Conplan
1130 Geli Moreira De Souza
1131 Logo For A Canoe Championship
1132 Luiz Olavo Fontes
1133 Editoro Globo

1134

1135

1136

1137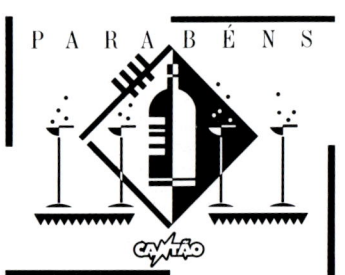

1138

1139

1140

1141

1134 Logo for a Surf Championship
1135 Health Food Restaurant
1136 Logo for a Surf Championship
1137 Birthday Announcement
1138 Sail Championship
1139 Ventana
1140 Logo for a Surf Championship
1141 Reflexo

1142

1143

1144

1145

1146

1147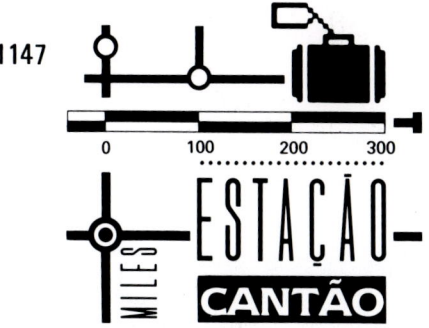

1148

1142 Solo
1143 Tatoosh
1144 Canto Vivo
1145 Logo for Radio Program
1146 Pack Way
1147 Cantao (Fashion Collection)
1148 Rogerio Martins/Sergio Liuzzi

1149

1150

1151

1152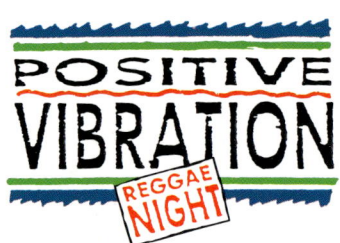

1153

1154

1155

1156

1149 Editora Globo
1150 Logo for a Cover Book
1151 Salada's
1152 Redley
1153 Salinas
1154 Lantao
1155 CRL
1156 Logo for Men's Clothing

1157
1158
1159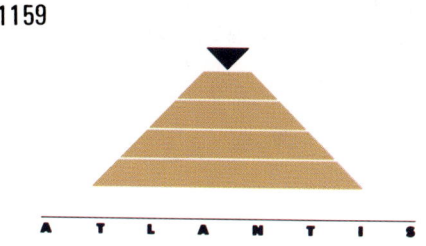
1160
1161
1162
1163
1164
1165

1157 Redley
1158 L.C. Barreto Producues Cinematograficos
1159 Atlantis
1160 Cantao (Logo for a Party)
1161 Typography For The New Year Calendar
1162 Galpao
1163 Chain of Clothing Stores
1164 Chain of Clothing Stores
1165 Chain of Clothing Stores

1166

1167

1168

1169

1170

1171

1172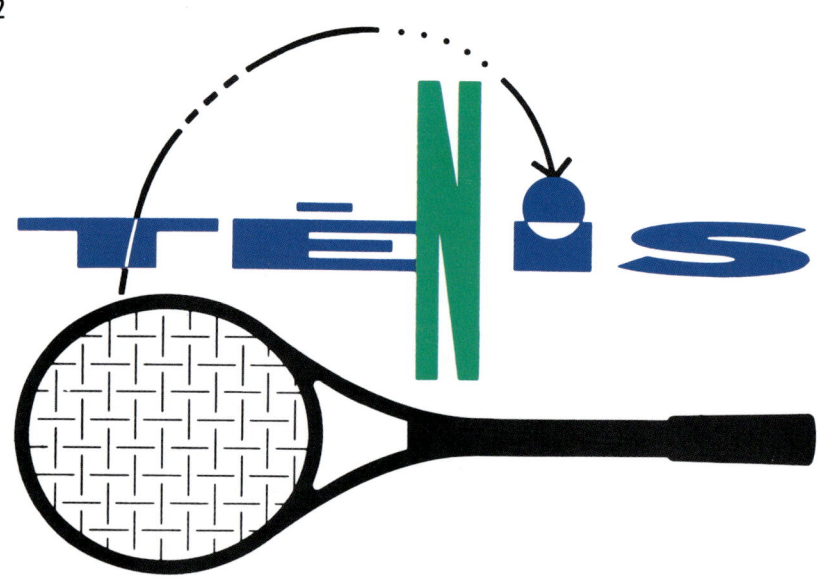

1166 Logo for a Party
1167 Logo for Sandals
1168 Redley
1169 Mango
1170 Label for Clothing
1171 Ettore
1172 Logo for a Tennis Championship

1173

1174

1175

1176

1177

1178

1179

1173 Novos Usos
1174 Nova Era
1175 Irwin Industrial
1176 Inter Casa
1177 Logo/Illustration for a Rock 'n Roll Group
1178 Salinas
1179 Rio Designer House

**Kinggraphic Advertising & Production Ltd.**
Hong Kong
1187–1196

1180
Shenzhen Information & Cultural Centre

1181

1182

1183

1184

1185

1186

1180 Shenzhen Information & Cultural Centre
1181 Wing On Culture Centre
1182 New-Star Superstore
1183 Lido Hotel
1184 IFPI
1185 Airlines Hotel
1186 Film Workshop

**Raymond Bennett Design**
Crows Nest NSW, Australia
1187-1196

1187

1188

1189

1190

1191

1187 Essential Software
1188 Zyliss Australia Pty. Ltd.
1189 Estoril Group
1190 Fielder Gillespie Limited
1191 Enacon

1192

1193

1194

1195

1196

1192 Transmission Products Pty. Ltd.
1193 The Office Wine Bar & Bistro
1194 Television Australia
1195 Beppis Ristorante
1196 Unifurn Pty. Ltd.

**Firma Design**
Sweden
1197-1203

1197

1198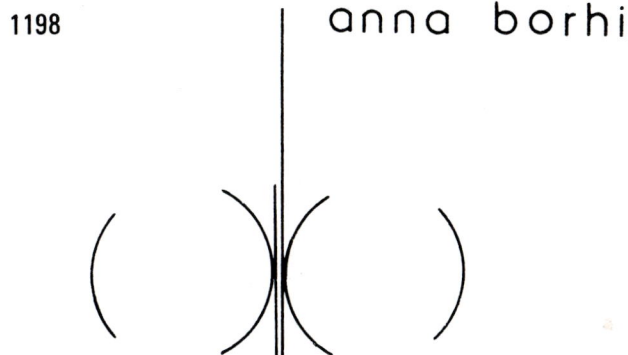

1199

1200

1201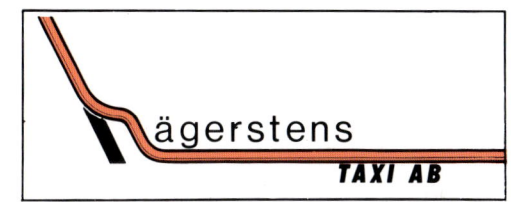

1202

1203

1197  Spotlight
1198  Anna Borhi
1199  Art Gallery
1200  Art Library
1201  Taxi Cab Co.
1202  Andras Makkai Design Management
1203  Reinholds

**Pentagram Design**
London W2 1LA England
1204-1243

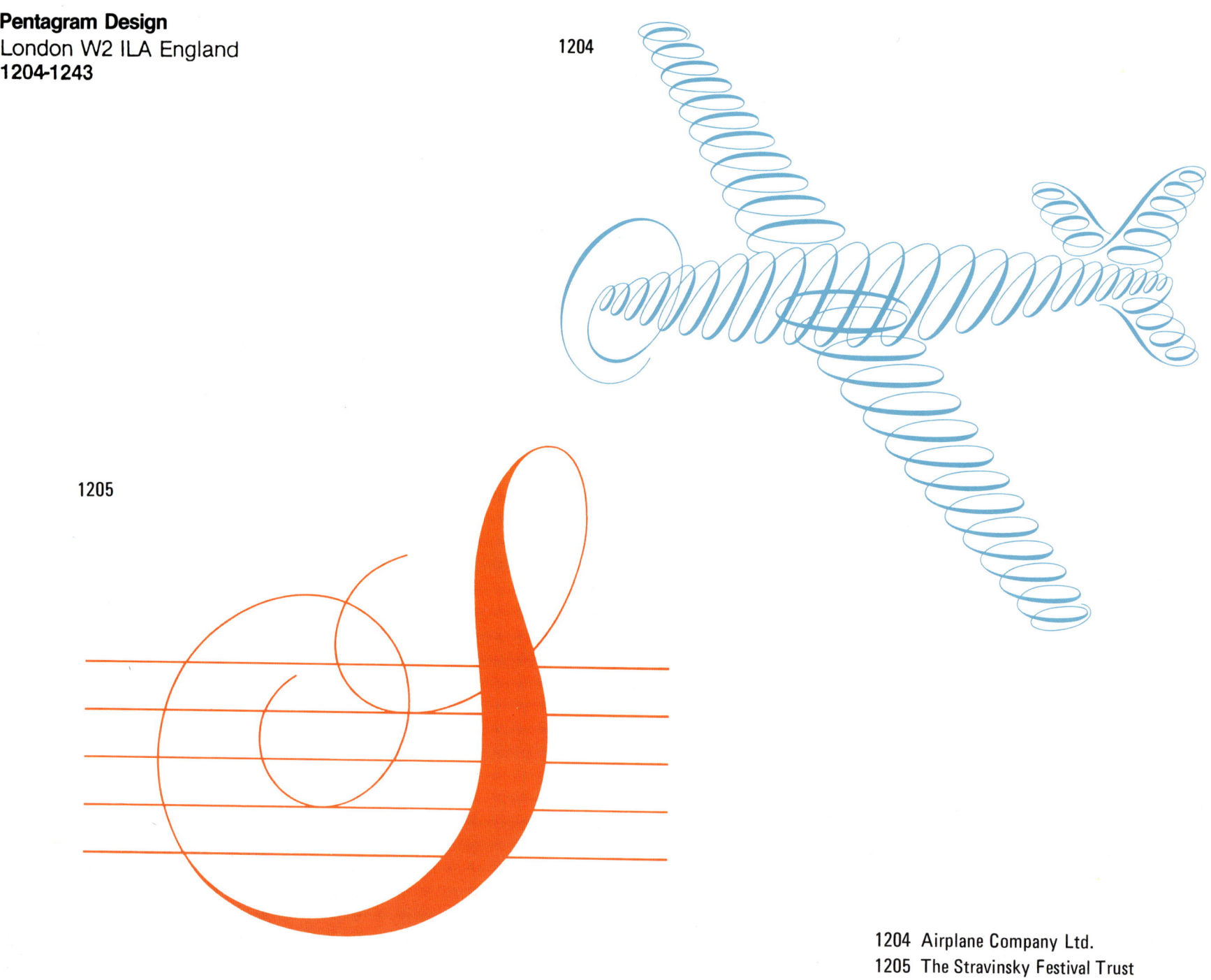

1204
1205

1204 Airplane Company Ltd.
1205 The Stravinsky Festival Trust

1206

1207

1208 MICHÈLE

1209

1210 Sketchley

1206 Matthews Goodman & Postlethwaite
1207 Biba
1208 Marks & Speners
1209 Cedric Lisney Associates
1210 Sketchley

1211

1212

1213

1214

1215

1211 National Book League
1212 Beeton & Tenant
1213 Face Photosetting Ltd.
1214 The Builder Group
1215 Design Council

1216

1217

1218

1219

1216 Saudi Arabian Government
1217 CApe Boards & Panels Ltd.
1218 British Telecom
1219 Watney Mann Truman Brewers

1220 Confederation of British Industry
1221 Gruppo Editoriale Electa
1222 Design & Art Directors Association
1223 Royal Institute of British Architects
1224 Gebruder Heinemann

1225 Commercial Bank of Kuwait
1226 Fire & Iron Gallery
1227 H. Nicoll
1228 Commercial Bank of Kuwait

1229

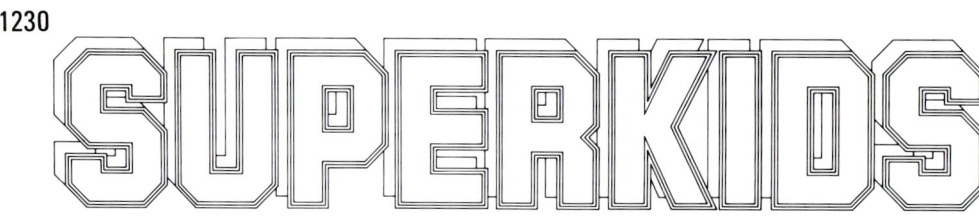
1230

1231

1232

1233

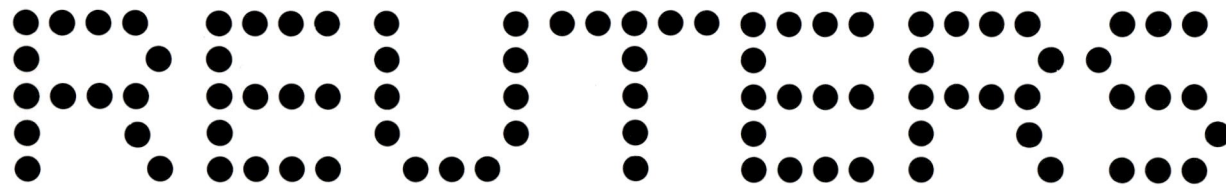
1234

1229 Standard Telephones & Cables
1230 Clarks Ltd.
1231 Viscom Visual Communications Ltd.
1232 Shiseido
1233 Faber & Faber Publishers
1234 Reuters Ltd.

1235 Haden

1236 [W logo]

1237 ARTHUR ANDERSEN & CO.

1238 Mg

1239 MILTON KEYNES

1235 Haden Ltd.
1236 Wood & Wood International Signs
1237 Arthur Anderson & Co.
1238 Mavity Gilmore
1239 Milton Keynes Development Corporation

1240

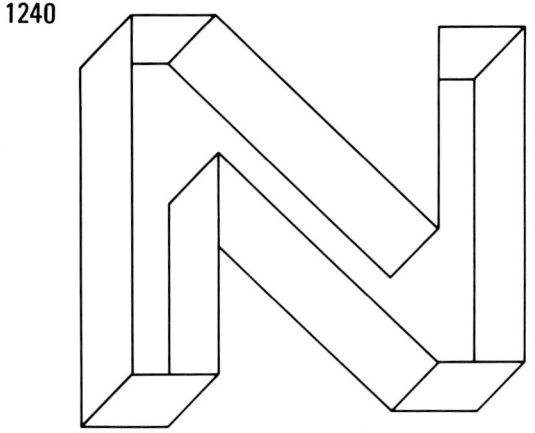

1241

1242

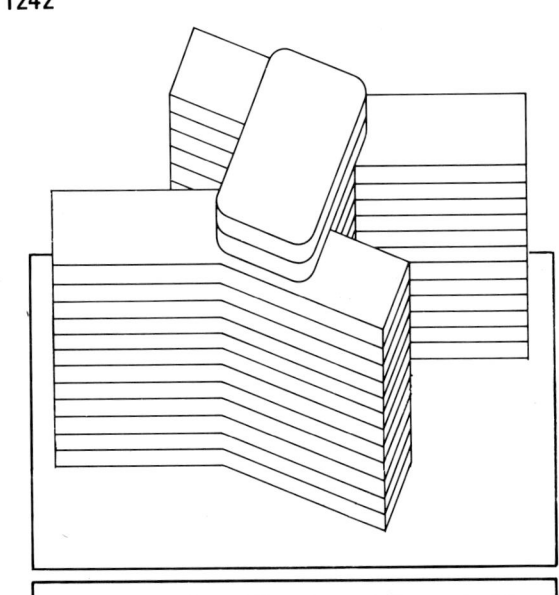

1240 Zinc Development Association
1241 Buro Happold
1242 Metropolitan Estates Property & Company

1243

1243 Association of Fashion Advertising & Editorial Photographers

**Sigla Sistema Globo
De Gravacoes Audio
Visuals Ltda.
1244-1249**

1244

1245

1246

1247

1248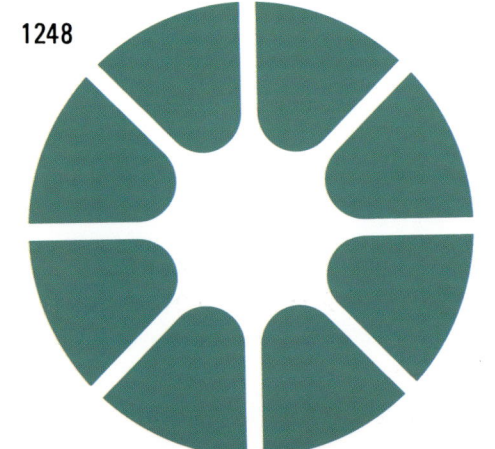

1249

1244  Hanoi-Hanoi
1245  Compact disc label
1246  Retro Music
1247  Project
1248  Goldmazon
1249  Via !!

**Marcela I. Alvarez Huerta**
Mexico
1250-1258

1250

1251

1252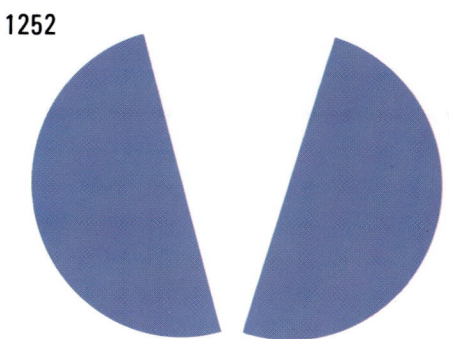

1253

1250 Linea de Tiendas de Campana Termicas
1251 Agente Profesional de Seguros/"Humberto Rodriguez"
1252 Farmacia "VIDA"
1253 Casa de Cambio Mercantil S.A. de C.V.

1254

1255

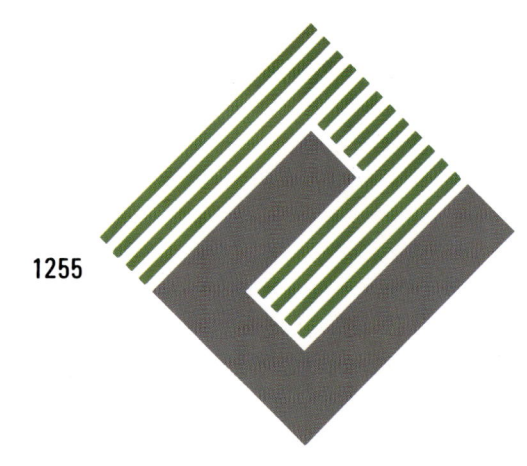

1256

1257

1254 Propuesta/Seguros Monterrey S.A. de C.V.
1255 Eficom S.C./Sistemas en Computacion
1256 Noe Valdes/Piloto Aviador
1257 "Clinica San Vicente"
1258 Disenador Grafico/Personal

**Anna i Jan Hollender**
art. graficy
Poland
**1259-1269**

1259

1260 　　1261

1262

1263 　1264 　1265 　1266

1267 　1268 　1269

1259　Remex
1260　Projekt
1261　Hortex
1262　Megat
1263　Dwood Ejem
1264　Depolma-Galeria
1265　MDM
1266　Narodowy Czyn/Pomocy Szkole
1267　Pekao
1268　desa
1269　Polski Monopol

**Leen Averink**
France
**1270-1273**

1270

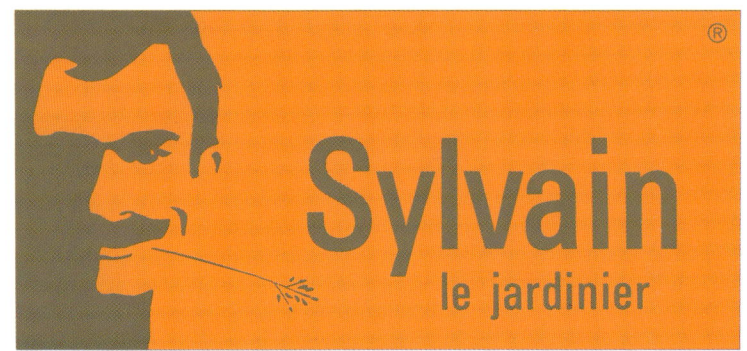

1271

1272

1270 Sylvain
1271 Projardin
1272 Trade Mark for Publicity Agency & Editor
1273 Institut Neerlandais